7

THE DAYSTAR VOYAGES

DANGERS OF THE RAINBOW NEBULA

GILBERT MORRIS
AND DAN MEEKS

MOODY PRESS
CHICAGO

This book is dedicated to my close friend and confidant, Matt Moyer. Although he would shake his head in disagreement—he is a man of God. I admire and respect him very much.

Matt, you've been my steadfast friend over the span of years. Through thick and thin. Through a little fatness, and a whole lot of leanness. Our friendship has remained solid. You, Jan, Rachel, and Tim will always be family to me. I praise the Lord for you and pray God's very best for you in the years ahead.

I love you brother—Dan

Characters

The *Daystar* ....an intergalactic star cruiser

The *Daystar* Space Rangers:
    Jerusha Ericson, 15....a topflight engineer
    Raina St. Clair, 14.......the ship's communications officer
    Mei-Lani Lao, 13 ....*Daystar*'s historian and linguist
    Ringo Smith, 14...........a computer wizard
    Heck Jordan, 15..........an electronics genius
    Dai Bando, 16..............known for his exceptional physical abilities

The *Daystar* Officers:
    Mark Edge ....*Daystar*'s young captain
    Zeno Thrax..................the first officer
    Bronwen Llewellen ....the navigator; Dai's aunt
    Ivan Petroski...............the chief engineer
    Temple Cole ....the flight surgeon
    Tara Jaleel ....the weapons officer
    Studs Cagney ....the crew chief

Contents

1
Jerusha's Problem

Jerusha Ericson took the face of her gigantic black dog between her hands and whispered, "You're the only one in the world I have to talk to, Contessa—the only one!"

The huge dog's brown eyes glowed with warmth and affection. Her heavy tail beat a tattoo as she rapped it against the deck of Jerusha's quarters.

Contessa was a super German shepherd, bred for intelligence. Her jaws were powerful enough to crush practically anything she could fasten them on. But as far as her mistress was concerned, the dog was nothing but gentleness. Now she lifted her head and, seeming to sense the distress in Jerusha's voice, said, "Wuff!"

"You'd like to help me, wouldn't you? But there's nothing you can do, old girl."

Jerusha Ericson, fifteen years old, had ash-blonde hair and very dark blue eyes. Her squarish face was strong. At five ten, she was athletic, and her intelligence equaled her physical abilities. An engineer aboard the *Daystar*, she could handle any mechanical problem that arose. But as she sat on the floor of her cabin, her back against the bulkhead, fondling the head of Contessa, sadness filled her.

She glanced around the cabin. It had become familiar to her. During her voyages with the *Daystar* Space Rangers, she had spent many hours here. But today there was less comfort in the familiarity of her surroundings.

Over the years, Jerusha had developed the habit of making even temporary quarters look and feel like home. Most of the books on her bookshelf were technical and engineering manuals. She kept up on the latest breakthroughs. Because of space limitations, the bookshelf was also the one place where she had the luxury of displaying family pictures. But to her dismay, the only picture she had there was one of Contessa and herself that had been taken on the planet Makon.

This place is feeling less like home than anywhere I've lived in a long time, she thought. She looked at the cushions that lay scattered around the room. She picked up one that she had purchased on Capella. The fabric was plush and soft and had a silky feel. The cushion was dark royal blue with vibrant yellow flowers floating across its surface. It stood out from the other cushions, which were mostly subdued earth tones. Each cushion in the room, including this new one, Jerusha considered her friend.

Jerusha looked about her quarters at the same level Contessa would see it—from the floor. She looked at the dominant pieces of furniture—the table and chairs. On the top of the table was her computer console.

"Computers!" she said to Contessa. "I've spent my life in front of them—and for what?"

Contessa leaned her head to one side, seemingly in wonder.

Jerusha got to her feet swiftly and with an easy motion. She walked over to the porthole and gazed out. She was always fascinated by the blackness of space. It was like smooth velvet spangled with literally millions of tiny burning points of light as far as the eye could see. She well knew that—farther than instruments could read—the universe that God had created stretched out infinitely.

With an impatient gesture, Jerusha turned and walked to her desk, where she threw herself down in her chair. She picked up her journal and a pen and began to write. Jerusha was so upset that she didn't know what the date was. But that didn't stop her from making an entry.

I don't know what's wrong with me—I feel absolutely terrible. I suppose I haven't gotten over our last mission to Capella. I woke up again last night having another horrible nightmare. I was being eaten alive by space locusts. It all came back to me then, as it has every night for the past week. Everyone is noticing I don't look well. Dr. Cole stopped me yesterday and asked me to come by for a visit. I know she thinks something's wrong physically. But it isn't physical. It's something else. Sometimes I feel like I'm surrounded by a vast army of giant insects, and I don't know what to do about it.

Contessa put her broad head into Jerusha's lap. Jerusha paused and casually stroked the dog's rough fur. Then she said out loud, "It's more than a fear of bugs troubling me. I don't know what it is, but for some time I've been waking up filled with resentment and anger, and I know that's not because of the monsters we saw on Capella!"

Her mind leaped suddenly to Capella's royal couple, Brutarius and his wife, Queen Anmoir. She had thought a lot about that family, and, not having close family of her own, had fixed on them as something she had missed out on.

She remembered how wonderful the royal family was. Both the suzerain and the queen had surrounded their beautiful daughter, Sanara, with love. Even Jerusha had sensed that love and oneness. Now, as she sat surrounded by the shell of the *Daystar*, she realized that something she had never known was very much alive in the suzerain's home on Capella.

Jerusha had always had a special gift of discernment. It was not that she was a mind reader, although some had accused her of that. It was that she had the ability to sense what people were like, often even when they tried to hide their thoughts and their emotions. During her time on Capella, it had given her a warm, pleasant, joyous feeling to understand the relationship that existed among those three.

Today, however, she was suddenly aware that her joy had turned into bitterness, and she admitted aloud, "I'm *jealous* of what they have!" She grabbed Contessa by the ears and shook her head roughly. "I've never had anything like that. The only thing I've had is you, Contessa."

The German shepherd growled deep in her throat. Suddenly she broke away and, rearing up, placed her paws on Jerusha's knees and licked her face.

Jerusha threw her arms around the giant dog, and tears formed in her eyes. "You're wonderful, Contessa, and I love you. But it's not the same thing as having parents and brothers and sisters."

Then she brushed Contessa aside and returned to the porthole. She stared out at the awesome sight of space with all of its diamondlike stars. And as she did so, she thought of something that had happened when she was a child.

Jerusha was an orphan. When she was five, the state had placed her in a foster home with two of the kindest people she had ever known. They gave her lots of love, and their home gave her a sense of security.

But one day, unannounced, a government social worker came by to check on Jerusha's progress. The woman strolled through the house, looking around. On Jerusha's dresser was a green leather Bible.

"And just whose is this?" the social worker demanded. "You know the rules!"

Her foster parents responded, "It used to be our daughter's many years ago. She used to read it when she was about Jerusha's age."

The social worker knelt down on one knee so that she could look eye to eye at Jerusha. Jerusha didn't like her angry look. "Have they been reading this book to you?" the woman asked Jerusha harshly.

"Yes." Her foster parents had told her it was always best to tell the truth.

The social worker became even more serious. "You must never read this book, or let anybody else read it to you. Do you understand?" She scowled at the foster parents, completed her checkup, and stormed out of the house.

The next day three men came and packed Jerusha's belongings and took her to their vehicle. The last thing she remembered was her foster mother shouting after her, "Jerusha, never forget about Jesus. Remember! Remember!"

Recalling all that was like salt in a raw wound to Jerusha. She stared blindly through the porthole. Yes, the Capella royal family had something she had never had, and Jerusha feared that she would never have it. She found herself trembling.

Contessa began to nudge her, whimpering, as though sensing the anguish in her mistress.

"It's all right, Contessa." Jerusha knelt and embraced the dog again. As Contessa licked her chin, Jerusha tried to laugh. She ran her hand over the massive dog's side and said, "You're getting fat! You're eating too many candy bars."

"Wuff!"

"You stay away from Heck Jordan! I know he's been feeding you his candy bars, and all that sugar just isn't good for you. Now, you mind me!"

Contessa seemed to have her feelings hurt at the sharpness of Jerusha's voice. She backed away, went across the room, and plumped down on the deck, flat on her stomach with her head between her paws. The dog's eyes followed Jerusha as she paced back and forth, talking to herself under her breath.

"I can't help thinking about Sanara. At least she had her family, and she had her bodyguard, Tramere. He was her friend and her protector, and he gave his life to save her from the space locusts. Why did she have a friend like that, and I don't have anybody?"

At this, Contessa raised her head. "Wuff! Wuff! Wuff!"

Jerusha glanced at the dog. "I know. I do have you, even if you can't talk, Contessa. But why did this have to happen to me? Why can't I have *somebody?* Why do I have to be all alone? Everybody else has a family."

This was not true, of course. Most of the other Space Rangers had no family either. Mei-Lani Lao, the cruiser's historian and linguist, had no more family than she herself. Ringo Smith had only recently found out that he had at least one parent, but this knowledge had brought nothing but pain. His father, he had discovered, was Sir Richard Irons, one of the most vicious space pirates in the galaxy. Dai Bando had his aunt— Bronwen Llewellen, the *Daystar*'s navigator—but neither Raina St. Clair, the communications expert, nor Heck Jordan, the electronics engineer, had any close relatives.

And then something happened that was unusual. Jerusha Ericson was a strong and self-reliant girl. She had fought her way through many difficulties before joining the Space Rangers and had since then proved herself courageous beyond question. Yet now her shoulders began to shake, and the emotion that rushed through her was a mixture of fear, anger, and despair.

Although Jerusha did not recognize it, as she sat weeping with only Contessa for comfort, she was opening her heart to that deadly emotion self-pity.

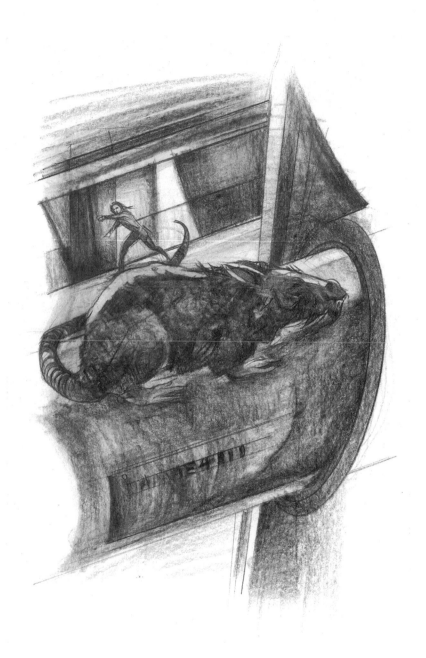

2

More Troubles

At thirteen, Mei-Lani Lao was the youngest person aboard the star cruiser *Daystar*. She was also the smallest. At only one inch over five feet, she weighed five pounds less than one hundred. Her warm brown eyes and round face usually wore an innocent expression.

Sitting comfortably in her cabin chair, Mei-Lani slowly turned the pages of a book yellowed with age. Her eyes rapidly took in the characters before her, which were in a most unusual language. Possessing a special gift for languages, the *Daystar*'s linguist and historian could learn a new one almost as easily as most people could learn how to play a new game. Her ability to analyze the ancient poets and philosophers, from both Earth and other places, was a source of constant amazement to the other Space Rangers and, indeed, to the captain and crew of the *Daystar*.

After a while Mei-Lani raised her eyes and just looked around the cabin, feeling a sudden sense of satisfaction and good fortune to have such fine quarters. Ever since she had been expelled from the Space Academy—as had most of the Space Rangers—Mei-Lani had desperately wanted a place of her own. And during the months that she and the others had been flying with Capt. Mark Edge, her quarters had been transformed from a Spartan cabin into a comfortable home.

Mei-Lani liked to collect unusual things—not just any things but those that had historical worth to her.

So her room was like a museum. A tragic fire had taken her parents' lives. One of the things that was salvaged from that fire was an ancient scroll from Earth's China. It was displayed against a bulkhead.

As her eyes continued moving about her room, Mei-Lani focused on her collection of multicolored crystals from Pluto. These were part of the first batch of crystals that had been brought back to Earth from the initial exploration expedition to that planet.

Now she left her chair to sit cross-legged on the bunk. "I'm glad I'm here," she whispered. "I'd rather be a *Daystar* Space Ranger than anything else in the world!"

A tap came at her door, and she said, "Come in." Then, as the door opened, her face broke into a smile. "Hello, Raina!"

"Hi, Mei-Lani. Are you busy?"

Without waiting for an answer, Raina St. Clair sat on a large cushion across from the younger girl and crossed her legs. Raina was one year older than Mei-Lani and one year younger than Jerusha. The three girls who made up the feminine part of the Space Rangers had been quickly drawn very close together. Both Mei-Lani and Jerusha had realized that Raina St. Clair was probably the most spiritually sensitive person on board the ship—except perhaps for Bronwen Llewellen, who was in a class by herself.

Raina had auburn hair, an oval face, attractive green eyes, and a dimple in her chin. She was not as athletic as the others and on their adventures outside the ship was constantly having to be helped.

Mei-Lani took in her friend's sober expression and said gently, "How are you today? I haven't talked to you lately."

"No. I've been . . . busy."

Something in Raina's hesitation caught Mei-Lani's attention. She knew her friend well. Raina was not a girl who could hide her feelings easily. She was usually very open and outgoing, warm and friendly, but now there was pain in her eyes and something about her set lips that told Mei-Lani all was not well.

"What's the matter, Raina? You're not yourself."

"Oh, I'm all right."

"Don't say that! This is Mei-Lani you're talking to!" Mei-Lani made a face. "I hate it when you ask someone how they are and they say, 'I'm fine,' and you know they're *not* fine."

Raina laughed shortly. "Well, it would be a rather awful thing if, when we ask people, 'How are you?' they really told us! I mean, if they told us they had a toothache, and that they weren't getting along with their best friend, and that they didn't have enough money to buy what they wanted. Most people don't really want to hear things like that."

"I guess that's right," Mei-Lani agreed. Still, she knew that something was disturbing the other girl. "But you know that friends exist so we can help each other. You can tell me your problem, whatever it is."

"You didn't tell *me* when you were worried sick about that breaking out on your face!"

"No, I didn't, and I should have! When we hold things in, they get worse." Mei-Lani started to say more, but then an idea came to her, and she made a quick guess. "I'll bet it has something to do with Dai Bando, doesn't it?"

A startled look swept across Raina's face. A slight flush began in her neck and then touched her cheeks. "I don't know what makes you think that."

"Well, you've always liked Dai, and you haven't been able to hide it too well." Another idea occurred to her, but she hesitated, not knowing whether to speak it out. "It can't be that you're jealous of Princess Sanara. Surely that's not it."

Raina blinked, and her flush grew even deeper. "Well, what if it is?" she said almost harshly. "Dai never looks at me the way he looked at that girl!"

Mei-Lani was surprised but not terribly so. Dai Bando was, without question, the best-looking boy that any of the three girls had ever seen. He had none of the technical skills of the rest of the Space Rangers, but his tremendous physical skills had saved them many times. He had strength, agility, speed—blinding quickness—and if he was afraid of anything, no one had ever found out about it.

"I don't think there's anything wrong with your liking Dai, but you shouldn't be jealous of Sanara. After all, nothing could ever come of their friendship. She's of the royal family. She'll be the next ruler of Capella one day. And also, she's just become a Christian—so you shouldn't have hard feelings toward her."

"I know. I know. But I can't help being—well, I guess *jealous* is the right word."

"Raina, even if Dai had never met Sanara, that wouldn't have changed anything. He's too young for anything serious, and so are you. Dai considers you a good friend, and that's what you are. And he's your friend, too, isn't he?"

Raina clearly was not happy. If she had wanted sympathy, she was not getting it from Mei-Lani. "I can't help it, Mei-Lani!" she complained. "I'm not physically strong. I don't have any stamina. I'm certainly not a princess!" Her face grew stiff as she whispered, "And I don't have any family. I've had to grow up all by myself. I just don't have any chance at all."

"I can't believe what you're saying!" Mei-Lani said.

She was shocked for she had always considered Raina to be a strong Christian—which she certainly was. But suddenly Mei-Lani realized that even the strongest Christians have their downsides, and obviously Raina was having one right now.

"You're not thinking right, Raina," she said. "You need to emphasize your strengths and not your weaknesses."

"*What* strengths?"

"You have lots of strengths! Nobody's better at communications than you are. Nobody aboard this ship knows so much about the encryption codes and structures."

"That's not such a big thing."

"Captain Edge thinks so. And so do we all. We all depend on you. The whole crew. We're like a big church here in a way—or a big family. We all have to depend on each other."

"It's not the same thing, Mei-Lani!"

Mei-Lani sensed that her friend was sinking deeper into emotional quicksand, and she said quickly, "Well, one thing you know is that your life belongs to the Lord Jesus. And at our last Bible study we went over the verse that says, 'We know that God causes all things to work together for good to those who love God, to those who are called according to His purpose.' You haven't forgotten that, have you?"

Shame crossed Raina's face. "No, I haven't," she whispered. "I haven't forgotten it."

"This whole thing isn't about family at all, Raina. It's about your feelings for Dai! And you've got to be so careful. Kids are so anxious to rush into relationships they're not ready for."

"Listen, you're only thirteen, and you're telling *me* how I ought to feel?" Raina got up and walked over to the porthole, where she stared out. "Guys like blue-eyed blondes who look like angels from heaven!" The words came out bitterly. She motioned to her reflection in the port glass. "All I see is a skinny, green-eyed brunette with an ugly widow's peak!"

"And that's silly, too! You're one of the prettiest girls I ever saw. But if you put all of your hope in looking good, you're bound to be disappointed, for there'll always be someone that looks a little better. But your main strength isn't that you're pretty, Raina. Though you certainly are."

"I don't *have* any strengths."

Seeing Raina so depressed, Mei-Lani thought, *I've got to get her mind off of Dai. He's got a special destiny from God, and not Raina, nor Sanara, nor anyone else, whether they're blonde or brunette, is going to come between Dai Bando and God's plans for him.*

Mei-Lani reasoned. "Listen to me. Dai's already said good-bye to Sanara. He won't see her again—at least not for the next few years. We're headed into an unknown part of the galaxy, and Captain Edge is just waiting for a message from Commandant Lee."

"I know that. I just can't pull myself together," Raina mourned.

Mei-Lani reached over to her bookshelf and pulled out an ancient book. She waved the book in the air as she spoke. "Look," she said. "Isn't it better just to be with Dai and the rest of the Rangers than be a girl that's always wishing she were somewhere else or even somebody else?" Mei-Lani pounded her index finger against the book cover.

"What girl are you talking about?" Raina asked.

But at that moment the intercom chimed, and Jerusha Ericson's voice came over the system. "Raina St. Clair, come by my quarters, please. At once!"

The voice sounded urgent, and Raina said, "I'll be right there, Jerusha."

"What do you suppose that is?" Mei-Lani asked. "She sounded very disturbed." She put the book back on the top shelf as Raina got up to leave. Then she picked up a sweater that she had thrown on the bed earlier. She folded the sweater in order to place it back in her drawer, but she was thinking about Jerusha's voice. "She sounded *very* troubled," Mei-Lani murmured. "I wonder what it is?"

Raina shrugged, then gave Mei-Lani a quick hug. "Thanks," she said as she bolted out the doorway into the corridor. The door closed behind her, leaving Mei-Lani alone.

Mei-Lani glanced at the clock. She was scheduled to help Bronwen Llewellen, and she saw that she was running late.

As Mei-Lani left her quarters, a flash of movement caught her eye. It was so quick that she almost missed it. Whatever it was, the thing was certainly alive, and she suddenly remembered that on a recent voyage the *Daystar* had become infested with a sort of purple rat.

"I hope it's not one of those ugly rats!" she muttered. "But it didn't look purple and hairy. It looked beige and white—and it was different from those purple rats."

She was puzzled, but time was short. "I'll have to be sure to tell Studs Cagney about it. He may have to become an exterminator as well as a crew chief."

3

Heck's Plan

Daystar's cargo bay was carefully designed. When flying out past the stars, any compartment that contained oxygen was very important, and the cargo bays were the largest areas aboard a spaceship.

Every cubic inch had to be accounted for. Supplies, extra equipment, inventory of all sorts were kept in sealed containers made of a durable plastic hybrid. When sealed, these were airtight as well as leakproof. There were several different-sized cargo containers, but all were silver with different-colored stripes on them. A blue-striped container contained engineering materials. A green-striped container held items for the chow hall. A red stripe meant computer equipment. Personal property containers had yellow stripes, and, due to cargo space limitations, these were few in number.

The cargo bay held rows and rows of these containers, stacked in racks twenty feet high. Each container rack was numbered on the *Daystar*'s cargo manifest. So if a computer circuit board was needed, the manifest would tell a grunt exactly which container rack held the needed item.

Studs Cagney was very proud of his cargo bay. He knew what was in every container and knew what container rack each was in—except for one container. Not knowing what was in that one yellow-striped container infuriated him.

Hector Jordan was paying no attention to his sur-roundings except to look over his shoulder with a furtive glance from time to time. He was searching for one very special cargo container, his prized possession on board. It contained a collection of tools and elec-tronic equipment that would have been the envy of any electronics department anywhere in the known galaxy.

But more than tools, it contained tiny amounts of the mineral tridium, which had been taken from the planet Makon. All the minerals had been secured in the *Daystar*'s security vaults, but it had been a simple mat-ter for an electronics expert such as Heck Jordan to bypass the alarm circuits.

Heck paused and thought about the great plan that he had concocted. At the age of fifteen, Heck was much overweight. He had candy bars concealed in every pocket and at strategic locations throughout the ship. Even now he pulled a chocolate bar out of an inner pocket, expertly ripped away the paper, and bit off half of it.

"Well," he muttered, "if my plan works, we'll see who's the head of the Space Rangers! All I have to do is keep borrowing tridium. The use of this mineral is going to revolutionize computer technology, and I want it all to myself! And besides that, if tridium does what I think it will, I can make a holographic virtual reality machine." Just the thought of living out his most secret fantasies excited him, and on top of that he would be rich beyond his wildest dreams.

A smile crossed Heck's face, and he chuckled deep in his chest. Popping the other half of the candy bar into his mouth, he nodded, thinking, *I'll be the boss of this ship then, and Capt. Mark Edge will have to come at my beck and call. And those girls, they'll be falling all over themselves when I get rich and famous.*

Satisfied with his thoughts, Heck reached for the handle of the toolbox container.

But at that moment, Studs Cagney appeared. He stopped and stared. A short, muscular man with thinning black hair and dark eyes, he had a rough manner about him, and now he spat out the question, "What are you doing there, Jordan?"

"Why—nothing, Chief!"

"What's in that container?"

"Oh, just some technical equipment. You wouldn't understand it if I tried to explain it."

"You think I'm stupid, huh!"

"Why, no!" Heck answered quickly, for the crew chief was a hot-tempered man at times. "I didn't mean that."

"I know what you meant, and I know what you think!"

"Now, really, Chief," Heck said, grinning broadly, "I don't try to be a crew chief. I don't see why you want to try to run the electronics part of the ship."

"You're up to something, Jordan. I can tell. In that fat head of yours is a brain that's always trying to get something out of somebody. You're a wheeler-dealer, and I know it!"

"Aw, Chief—"

"Don't 'aw, Chief' *me!*" Studs said. Then a memory seemed to come to him, and it brought a smile to his face. "I hear Lieutenant Jaleel really wiped up the floor with you last week."

Heck frowned, remembering how the weapons officer had pounded him until he felt black and blue all over. She gave martial arts lessons to all the Space Rangers but seemed to take particular delight in roughing up Heck. He was so overweight and his reactions so slow that she had no trouble bouncing him against the walls of the workout room like a rubber ball.

"Aw, she never did like me. She'll be sorry someday."

"What do you mean by that?" Studs demanded. "You gonna throw her off the ship into deep space?"

"Well, I'd like to!"

"Won't hurt you to get roughed up a little bit. It's a good thing for a young man to bear the yoke in his youth. That's what the Bible says."

Heck gave the muscular crew chief an odd look. "Dai Bando's been reading you the Bible again?"

"Reading it to me, nothing! I'm reading it for myself!"

"Are you going to be a Christian, then?"

"There's worse things to be, and I've been most of them."

Indeed, Studs Cagney had come up the hard way, but young Dai had been a great influence on him. When Dai first came aboard, Studs tried to thrash him, only to find out to his amazement that the boy's strength, speed, and agility made this impossible. Failing to thrash him, he had given him the dirtiest jobs on the ship, hoping this would humiliate him.

But it had not, and Studs became a secret admirer of Dai Bando. Now, the two of them spent some time talking together almost every day. Dai liked to hear Studs's stories about his adventures in space, and Studs had grown interested in Dai's religious beliefs.

"You want a candy bar, Chief?"

"No, I don't want a candy bar! Get on with your work!" The crew chief turned away abruptly.

But at that moment, Heck heard Dai's whistling, and he said, "You'd better be nice to me, or I'll have Dai give you a going-over!"

"You think he'd pay any attention to you? You're going to tell me the truth about what's in that container sooner or later."

As Studs left, Heck wiped the sweat from his brow. "That was a close one," he muttered. He reached up and strained at the container, which was high over his head. He pulled it out a little way, but it was still too high. "If I pull it all the way out," he mumbled, "it'll fall and crush me. It weighs a ton."

Now standing on his toes, Heck tried desperately to control the box. But it was extremely heavy, and he stood struggling with it in frustration.

Dai Bando broke off his whistling. "Hey, Heck! What's coming down?" Dai usually whistled or sang Welsh melodies. Both his voice and his whistling ability were phenomenal. The melodies were rich and pure and sweet, and everyone on the ship seemed to look forward to hearing them.

Dai Bando was sixteen, the oldest of all the Space Rangers. He had hair as black as a raven's wing, and his eyes were so dark that they seemed at times to have no pupils. He had a build much like that of a galactic Olympic gymnast.

He was a quiet young man as a rule, however, much aware and rather sad that he was not as technically minded as the rest of the Rangers. He had, as a matter of fact, been included among the ensigns only because his aunt, Bronwen Llewellen, had insisted on it. Captain Edge quickly learned from observation that the boy, though not a computer expert or an electronics genius, was a worthy member of the crew.

"Hey, Dai, give me a hand, will you?"

"Sure. What do you need, Heck? You want that big box down?"

"Yeah, I could do it myself, but I'm not quite tall enough."

Dai did not smile although he must have known the weight of the container would simply demolish

Heck. "Here, let me help." He put down the box he had been carrying, reached up, and lifted the heavy case containing Heck's secret equipment as if it were packed with Ping-Pong balls. He placed it on the floor, saying, "There. Anything else?"

Heck's face was still red from effort. He secretly resented Dai. The three young ladies of their company obviously admired Dai much more. He had thought more than once, *Wait'll I get my virtual reality machine on the market! I'll be rolling in dough then. We'll see who the girls come to, Dai Bando!*

Heck wiped his face with a brilliant yellow handkerchief. His uniform was required, but, being color-blind, he often picked accessories that clashed with it. He sometimes looked somewhat like a walking rainbow, except not as well matched.

"You know, Heck. We ought to work out together some. You're a little bit overweight."

"I don't want to hear about it!"

"Well, you really should take care of yourself. It's not too hard, either. We could do it together."

Heck well knew that Dai worked out every day, even though he obviously didn't need it. He also knew that Dai watched what he ate, while Heck ate everything he could get his hands on, especially sweets. Life without sweets would have been like no life at all for Heck Jordan.

Dai said, "What do you say? Meet me tomorrow in the training room, and we'll start working out. We'll start real slow. I promise."

Heck Jordan saw the earnestness in Dai's dark eyes and found himself liking the boy despite his envy of Dai's physique and strength. "Well, OK. I guess a little bit wouldn't hurt. But you've got to keep Tara Jaleel away from me."

"Don't worry. We'll go early before she gets there."

"OK. Well, thanks for the help."

"Don't mention it."

As Dai left the cargo bay, Heck looked about quickly, making sure that no one was coming. Then he opened the box with the special key that he kept around his neck. He removed some tools and circuit boards that he needed for his new project, plus some of the tridium crystals. He closed the box then, shoved it back against the bulkhead, and quickly left for the fuel cells, which were located at the very rear of the hold.

As he strode along, Heck hummed a little tune, and a smile came over his face. He was thinking about the day when he would be Admiral Hector Jordan, Commander of the Star Fleet and Master of the Galaxy.

4

Friends Share with Friends

One of the things that Raina liked most about the *Daystar* was the unlimited amount of melon nectar drinks that were available. Everyone on board loved the bubbly drink that tasted like watermelon and peaches. Dr. Cole had even pronounced it healthful to drink. Studs Cagney was ordered by Captain Edge to stock it and keep a good supply on board. No one ever grew tired of it.

In Jerusha's quarters, Raina and Jerusha sat down, ready to enjoy tall glasses of frosty nectar. Contessa immediately walked to the door and began clawing at it with one large paw.

"That dog!" Contessa's mistress shook her head. "If she's in, she wants out. If she's out, she wants in." Getting to her feet, she opened the door, and the German shepherd trotted out quickly. Jerusha sat down across from Raina again and said, "For a long time, Contessa was the only friend I had, Raina."

"She's a fine animal. I'll bet there's not a smarter dog in the whole galaxy—or one that loves her mistress more, either."

"I suppose that's true." Jerusha took a sip of the drink and brushed her hair back from her forehead. Both girls were off duty and were wearing leisure clothes. "I've talked Contessa's ears off, but I asked you to come because I need somebody that can talk back to me. I've spent a lot of time blowing off steam to a dog that has no idea what I'm talking about."

Raina nodded and sipped her fruit drink. "I know exactly what you mean, because I've been sharing things with Mei-Lani. But you know, Mei-Lani is just a little too young to understand what goes on in the heart of an older woman."

Jerusha smiled. "I think we've got a similar problem. Not the same but similar."

"What's that, Jerusha?"

"Sanara, of course."

At the word *Sanara*, Raina felt her face stiffen and her eyes fill with tears.

"Why, Raina—"

"You don't know how it hurt when Dai gave Sanara all his attention—when it was attention from him that *I* wanted!" Raina rushed on for some time, finally saying with a gasp, "That girl's nothing but a flirt!"

Jerusha obviously could tell that she was terribly upset.

"Raina," she said quietly, "Sanara's a Christian now, a sister in the Lord. And as for her being beautiful and being a member of royalty—she didn't create that for herself. God gave it to her."

"But why did He give all that to her and so little to me?"

"This isn't like you at all, Raina!" Jerusha said, sharply now. "Besides, *I'm* the one who needs help here. I'm the one who called for *you*, remember? *Listen to me!*"

Raina was startled, but she wisely chose to be quiet. She listened indeed as Jerusha began to pour out her problem. In fact, she couldn't have gotten a word in edgewise. And as she listened, feeling somewhat ashamed of herself, Raina started to sense that Jerusha's problem with Sanara was far greater than her own. It touched on things in Jerusha much deeper than

Raina's own romantic pangs over Dai Bando. She also saw that she and Jerusha must help each other.

Raina waited until she got a chance to break in. Then she said softly, "Jerusha, as Christians we all believe that God is our Father."

"I know that!"

"I'm sure you do, but think of it like this—" Raina went on quietly. "We belong to *His* family now. Everyone who belongs to Him is related to each other in a way that we could not be physically. Now, it happens that Sanara has had an almost perfect family setting, but many families aren't like that. I had one friend whose sister was so mean to her that she grew to hate her. But we mustn't let that happen in the family of the Lord. I see now that, if people are Christians, no matter how different they are, or how much they get on our nerves, or how much they have that we don't— they're still our brothers or sisters in the Lord. And that's the way we both need to learn to think about Sanara."

Suddenly, Jerusha began to talk about the hurts and disappointments of her childhood. The emotional baggage that had built up inside her over the years poured out of her. Like a pressure-filled volcano, she spewed out the harsh feelings, the bitterness, and the years of loneliness that she had kept under lock and key in her heart.

And now Raina better understood. Finally she asked, "Do you blame God for all this, Jerusha?"

Jerusha instantly closed her mouth and stared wildly at her friend. Then she rose, threw herself across the bed, and began to sob. When Raina sat beside her and placed a hand on her shoulder, she gasped, "I know my feelings are wrong, but I just couldn't help myself. I *have* blamed God. He could have planned things better for me—the way He did for Sanara."

Raina gently rubbed her friend's shaking shoulders and waited for the storm of weeping to leave. It was a time such as she and Jerusha had never experienced together. They had gone through danger and had become close friends, but it was as if for the first time each of them had torn away the curtain from her heart.

"I don't know what to tell you. I'm no one to be giving advice," Raina said sadly. "But what I think you should do is talk to Bronwen Llewellen about this. I don't think there are any easy answers that she'll give you. Only the Lord can do that, but Bronwen's closer to God than anyone I know."

Jerusha started to answer, but at that moment there was a scratching at the door. She scrambled to her feet, wiped at her eyes with a handkerchief, took a deep breath, and walked over to open it.

Contessa was back. The dog came in and looked up at both girls. When Jerusha sat down, she lay down at her feet.

Neither Jerusha nor Raina, who were watching the dog, noticed the small beige-and-white animal that had sped through the door as it closed and hid under the bed. If the two Space Rangers had realized what danger they were in, they would have fled the room immediately.

The animal was a borator. It was not much larger than a small kitten. Hairless and almost blind, the creature burrowed through the ground on the planet Capella, looking for different roots and minerals to consume. If it had to bore through rock to get at crystals, the borator would secrete a highly caustic acid that could burn through solid rock. The crystals it found would be dissolved by the acid and then eaten by the borator. What made the borator so dangerous was its bite. It would inject its victim with acid, which would cause instant circulatory failure. The creature had stumbled its way into a gold mine—the *Daystar*.

Raina and Jerusha talked until they were both emotionally exhausted.

But life had to go on. "I've got to report for duty at Communications," Raina said at last. "I have to go change into my uniform."

"I'm glad you came," Jerusha said warmly, though her face was drawn. "Thank you."

"Promise me you'll go talk to Bronwen."

"I will, although I don't see what good it will do."

"I don't either, but when I've had problems, I've found that Bronwen Llewellen is the one to talk to. I'll see you later."

"All right. Later."

Jerusha waited until the door closed, then reached down to pat Contessa. She realized that she was wallowing in self-pity but at the same time did not know what to do about it. "Contessa, you're still the only real family I've got."

"Wuff! Wuff!" Contessa sat up at once and began to try to lick Jerusha's face.

"No, you'll smear my lipstick!"

And then Jerusha began to sniff the air. "What's that I smell?" she murmured. She looked down at Contessa. "You're the one with the super sense of smell. Don't *you* smell anything?"

Contessa cocked her head to one side, and as Jerusha moved about the room trying to locate the peculiar odor, the dog too began sniffing. Finally she sniffed at a floor vent located by the bed.

Jerusha got down on her stomach and peered into the vent. "Nothing down there, Contessa."

The dog sat down, cocked her head again, and said, "Wuff!" It was the only thing she could say. Perhaps, if she could have talked, she might have told her mistress much more than this.

5

A Master at Work

Ringo Smith was perhaps the most modest of all the Space Rangers. He was a quiet fourteen-year-old with brown hair and very light hazel eyes, and was slightly built.

Despite his appearance and modesty, Ringo was a computer genius. What took others months or even years to learn about the computer, Ringo simply soaked up effortlessly.

Sitting in his cabin, feet propped up against the pillows on his bunk, he was surrounded by drawings, diagrams, and books, all related to computers. Mei-Lani had once asked him if he ever read poetry or novels, and he had looked at her with astonishment, answering, "No. They're not as much fun as computers."

Ringo lifted his eyes to the porthole. He always enjoyed the sight of outer space. He found the darkness somehow comforting, for it was highlighted by brilliant points of light—stars, comets, whole galaxies thrown out across the curtain of space.

Until recently, Ringo had never understood why he found space so pleasurable. It had finally come to him that space had stability and posed no problems for him.

The best thing that had happened to Ringo had been to escape the state orphanage and get into the Space Academy. However, even memories of that part of his life were not altogether pleasant. He had been so shy that he had made few friends. All the rest of the cadets seemed to have family and background. He had felt inferior for not having the same sort of family life as the others. And then he had been expelled for his Christian beliefs. It had seemed the end of the world to him.

Ringo picked up a drawing of the special computer that he had been working on and tried to focus on it. But instead of the lines of the circuits, a face swam into his vision. It was a hard face, handsome in a way, but with cruel eyes, and Ringo recognized instantly the face of his father, Sir Richard Irons.

Another unpleasant memory! He had learned on their last journey into space that Sir Richard Irons, the greatest space pirate of the galaxy, was his father! The scene flashed before his eyes, and he could hear again his father's harsh voice telling how he had done away with his wife and was perfectly willing to do away with this son of his.

Ringo stood to his feet, scattering the papers and books. He poured himself a glass of melon nectar, which he drank quickly to ease his dry throat. "Better to be in space," he said, "with no parents at all than have *him* for a father!"

A fast knock sounded, and, startled, Ringo turned toward the door. "Who could that be?" he muttered. He did not have many visitors.

But when he spoke the word that caused the door to slide back into the bulkhead, he saw Heck Jordan standing in the corridor, grinning at him. "Come in, Heck," he said and went back to sit on his bunk.

Heck Jordan sat beside him. Ramming his hand into one of his many pockets, he brought forth two candy bars and handed one to Ringo. "Here. You look like you need some nourishment. Eat hearty! It'll keep your strength up!"

"Keep my strength up for what?" Ringo asked listlessly. His memories always depressed him. He wished that he had some *good* times to look back on. Of course, now he was a member of the crew of the *Daystar*, and he had good friends among the young Space Rangers, but somehow he still felt alone.

Heck chattered away nonstop, apparently with nothing on his mind, but Ringo sensed that *something* was there. And then Heck said, "You still stuck on Raina St. Clair, are you, Ringo?"

"I never said I was."

"Well, you don't have to say so. The way you watch her, anybody with any sense would know that you're crazy about her."

"She's a fine girl . . . and she's cute," Ringo said defiantly. Suddenly the candy bar was tasteless, and he tossed it down on the table. "You didn't come to talk about Raina, did you?"

"Well, as a matter of fact I did—in a way." Heck's voice was rather careless, but something about the tone of it caught at Ringo. "You see, friends have to stick together, and we're friends, aren't we?"

"I guess so, Heck, but I don't want to talk about Raina."

"Well, you don't have to talk. Just listen." Heck leaned forward. His eyes were bright with excitement. "How would you like to have a lot of good times with Raina?"

"No chance of that."

"Well, maybe not right now in real life, but how about a holographic virtual reality machine?"

"Those things don't work. I tried one once."

"Hey, man, they never worked until *now*. But that was before Heck Jordan came onto the scene." Leaning forward again, he said in a whisper, "I've figured out a way to make a reality machine that will put all others out of business." His voice filled with excitement, and he started into a highly technical explanation.

Ringo stared at him blankly and finally shook his head. "I don't understand all of this."

"You don't have to understand it," Heck said importantly. "I've got all the details worked out. Heck Jordan's in charge, but I do need a little help."

"Help for what?"

"Well, I need a computer expert, and who is more expert than my friend Ringo Smith!"

"What do you need a computer for?" In spite of himself, Ringo was interested, as he always was when someone mentioned anything to do with computers. "What kind of computer do you need? The ship is full of them."

"Listen, Ringo, I need a beefed-up supercomputer with the fastest processor in existence. I'm right on the verge of discovering a way to focus the tridium crystals and cause them to do something that's never happened before in the history of man."

"To do what?"

"I've found out a way to interface with brain waves."

Ringo studied Heck Jordan's round face. Then he shook his head before letting out a short laugh. "That's impossible!"

"It is for everybody else, but it won't be for us. I just need a little help with some computer stuff. I can do the electronics and the schematics, but I've got to have your help."

"I don't think it's possible! You're dreaming!"

Again, Heck began to talk rapidly—not so much this time about the technical side of building the virtual reality machine as about the way it would work. And

Heck was a persuasive talker. He would have made a good used space freighter salesman if he had chosen to go in that direction.

Ringo was beginning to be interested in the details.

"So, just imagine this. You and Raina out ice skating, say. Just you and her. You've got your hands crossed, and you're sailing around on that smooth, white ice, and around you there are beautiful mountains. And she's looking at you! She's smiling at you, and she's squeezing your hands. How would you like something like that?"

As a matter of fact, Ringo would have liked it very much. Just the *idea* of skating with Raina was enticing. "But I can't even skate," he muttered.

"Can't even skate? Maybe not on a real rink, but in my machine you can skate like a champion. That's the beauty of this, don't you see? You can live any dream you want with anybody you want. Why, you and Raina could go hang gliding together. You could go canoeing in the South Sea islands. You could go swimming in the Caribbean. Wouldn't that be something—diving among the reefs?" Heck went on and on. "What do you say, buddy? I'll cut you in on the profits, too. Say one percent."

That was exactly the kind of split that Ringo might have expected. Ninety-nine percent for Heck and 1 percent for him. However, Ringo was not interested in the money. He said, "Tell me what kind of computer you need."

"Now you're talking!" Heck slapped Ringo on the back. He waved his hands around excitedly. He grabbed up sheets of paper and began drawing a diagram.

Ringo sat, his eyes fixed on his chubby visitor.

"Well, do you think you can do it?" Heck finally asked.

"I don't know. I can try."

"That's good, buddy. Now come on. I want to show you how it's going to work."

"Where are we going?"

"Going to the fuel cells."

"The fuel cells!" Ringo got to his feet and followed Heck down the corridor. On the way they passed crew members, who greeted them, but when they neared the stern of the *Daystar*, they found that section of the ship totally uninhabited.

Ringo said nervously, "I don't like to get this close to these fuel cells. They're dangerous."

"Aw, don't be an old woman!" Heck said. "Come on."

As Ringo followed him into the very midst of the huge reactors, the hair on his neck stood on end. The fuel cells were highly volatile and indeed dangerous, and he always kept as far away from them as possible. In addition to this, he was afraid that he and Heck would be discovered.

"If Captain Edge catches us back here, he'll throw us into space!" he protested.

"Aw, who's gonna tell? Nobody here. Nobody ever comes here. That's why it's safe. Now I'm going to show you something."

Heck led him to his new, holographic contraption, and Ringo assessed the makeshift-looking blue pod. Somehow Heck had managed to disassemble and then splice together several large cargo containers.

When they walked in through the pod's only door, he saw that the interior was the same blue as the exterior. Heck had placed a single chair in the center of the room.

Ringo stooped down to examine the chair's mechanism. "Why, this is not a chair at all!" he said admiringly. "You've put a lot of thought into this." He glanced over his right shoulder at Heck. "You beat all! How did you manage to get all this back here without Ivan spotting you?"

"I'll admit it wasn't easy. I not only had to disassemble the containers and slip them back here a piece at a time, but I also had to adjust the cargo manifest so Ivan wouldn't miss them."

Ringo was shaking his head back and forth as he continued to examine Heck's invention. "How does this work?" he asked, while feeling one of the chair arms.

"As you can see, this appears to be just a chair, but actually—after you sit in it—it clamps onto your body." Heck pointed out the different mechanisms. The clamps were bronze colored and equipped with golden sensor units at the ends of them.

"This top clamp looks a little different from the others," Ringo noted questioningly.

Heck lifted the device. "This clamp closes gently on either side of your neck." He held the clamp a little higher. "The tridium is implanted in the sensor circuits. The clamp snugs the sensors to your neck just above your shoulders. See? The rest of the clamps have tridium sensors, too, and they all interface with the neck sensors." Heck walked around the pod, waving his arms at the walls and ceiling. "The tricky part is interfacing the tridium sensors with the holographic unit."

"I can believe that!" Ringo responded. "It would take a powerful computer to relay the nerve impulses from the brain and translate them into electronic impulses a computer would understand." He stood with his hand to his chin. His eyes looked straight at the ceiling while he tried to envision the whole computer process.

"That's why I need you, buddy!" Heck exclaimed.

Ringo was well aware that Heck had a different definition of the word *buddy* than he did.

"I've worked out most of the details myself," Heck hurried on. "But I need your computer ingenuity to work out the details with the hardware and software bugs. You're the absolute best computer man for the job—a job that will wind up making us both rich." He looked closely at Ringo's face and added, "And you'll be able to go anywhere you want with Raina."

Ringo said nothing for a few moments. Then he came to a conclusion. "There's no way we can make this work."

"Why not?" Heck asked hotly.

"Power." Ringo knew this contraption would need a lot of power.

Heck put an arm across his shoulders. "Power we have plenty of—and all the power we'll ever need, too!" Heck whispered just loud enough for Ringo to hear him.

"How?"

Heck led him out through the door of the pod and then to the very rear section of the cruiser. Here huge laser cables connected Heck's pod directly to one of the main fuel cells.

Heck said triumphantly, "I didn't have enough power to get the job done, so I connected the equipment directly to the fuel cells."

"Are you *crazy?* This could get us both court-martialed!"

Heck only laughed. "I needed more energy for this than I could get approved by Captain Edge. Besides, I want to keep it all a secret. If it went through the normal power grids, the cat would be out of the bag."

The two argued back and forth, and the argument revolved mostly around how many rules they were breaking.

"Heck," Ringo exclaimed, "the fuel cells are the very lifeblood of the ship! All of our lives depend on them." He waved a hand near the surface of the closest fuel cell. The energy that pulsed through the cell felt like that inside a gigantic dynamo. "If we were to miscalculate our figures by a centimeter, the fuel cells would blow up. This is far too dangerous. Goodness, Heck, we aren't even supposed to be *in* here! This area is strictly off limits!"

But Heck brushed all Ringo's protests aside. "Look. If you want to get somewhere in this world, you got to take a chance. We're just borrowing some equipment, and we're borrowing a little of the power. Why, Captain Edge will be proud of us both when we come out with our machine."

"I don't think so. You know how he is about going around the rules."

"Look," Heck said patiently, "the scientists in Intergalactic Command have never had tridium crystals to work with before, and you know there's no other mineral in the known galaxy like this stuff. The old virtual reality technology used silicon crystals, and they were never able to do the job. They could never hook up with the awesome power of the brain directly!"

The deep humming of the mighty star engines formed a chorus in Ringo's ears as he listened to Heck, who became absolutely eloquent. Ringo knew, however, that Heck could always become eloquent when he was getting something for himself or when he wanted someone to do something that wasn't exactly right. Ringo felt resistant. And yet, to be with Raina even in a dream was more than he had ever hoped for.

"This machine is going to be a gateway into whole new worlds, into the depths and the heights of the mind, Ringo," Heck said grandly. "There's no end to the possibilities of tridium—it's a miracle mineral!"

"If we don't get caught."

"Don't think negative thoughts." Heck waved his hands around yet again, then reached into his pocket. "Here, let's have a couple of candy bars to celebrate our new partnership!"

6

The Rainbow Nebula

Capt. Mark Edge was the last to enter the bridge conference room of the *Daystar*. This room was also used by Captain Edge as a war room if the situation warranted. A large white enamel table dominated the center of the room, and it was surrounded by chairs covered with Dernof leather dyed the same color as the table.

Edge took his seat and glanced around at his officers. They included First Officer Zeno Thrax, Chief Engineer Ivan Petroski, Medical Officer Temple Cole, and Navigator Bronwen Llewellen. He felt a sense of satisfaction, thinking, *Not many space fleet captains have a senior staff as capable as this one. But I'm not going to let them know it. They might get arrogant, and if anyone's going to be arrogant, it'll be me.*

"I want a full report from each one of you!" Edge snapped. "You first, Zeno!"

Zeno Thrax, the first officer, was a perfect albino, having white hair and colorless eyes. He was rather chilling to look at, but the man really had a warm heart. He came from the planet Mentor Seven, where there was nothing but mines and all the people lived underground.

Zeno's voice was crisp and businesslike. "We are headed directly toward the Rainbow Nebula." He turned toward the forward port and pointed to the immense star system lying in their path. "It has an unusual designation by Earthlings. They call it the 'Bermuda Triangle' of the galaxy."

"Bermuda Triangle! What is that?" Edge interrupted.

The albino looked at him with translucent eyes. "I've researched the term, and the only reference I can find for it comes from Earth's twentieth century."

Thrax walked over to the chart board and drew a rough likeness of Earth's Western Hemisphere. Then he pointed to a section of the ocean. "This area of the Caribbean Sea is roughly the shape of a triangle, and it is situated very near the islands named Bermuda and Puerto Rico—and also the state of Florida, located on the North American continent. Hence the term 'Bermuda Triangle' originated."

"But that doesn't tell me what it means!" Edge walked over to the chart board and stood next to him.

"This area," Thrax said, pointing again, "had an ominous reputation due to the number of planes and oceangoing ships that disappeared in its waters without explanation." Then Zeno walked to the port and looked toward the Rainbow Nebula. "Exactly the same reputation the Rainbow Nebula has. Many spaceships have flown in the area of the Rainbow Nebula and have never been seen again. Just like the ships and planes in the 'Bermuda Triangle,' they disappeared without explanation." The first officer returned to his chair.

The air in the conference room suddenly seemed very chilly. Everybody in the room sat silent as they realized that they were headed toward a very dangerous part of the galaxy. No one wanted to disappear without explanation.

"Why in the name of Jupiter's moons," Ivan Petroski objected, "do we have to go into that part of space?"

Petroski had a dwarf's body, but he was an excellent engineer. Now his voice was angry as he insisted, "We'd be better off to face a couple of Denebian war cruisers than to jump into that Rainbow Nebula. Nobody even knows what's there!"

"Hold your questions for the time being, Chief!" Edge said sharply. "I want to get this status report complete by the time Commandant Lee contacts me with further orders. All I know right now is that the *Daystar* is to proceed toward the Rainbow Nebula."

Ivan Petroski grunted and slumped back in his chair. There was something comical about such a small individual having such a temper, and laughter broke out around the table. The chief engineer was so diminutive that he did not present much of a threat.

Edge put up with the laughter for a moment. Then, "All right. Knock it off!" he said. "Ivan, no disrespect was intended. Don't pay any attention to them."

"I don't!" Petroski said crossly.

"What about battle damage, Zeno?"

Thrax spoke up at once. "We received minor damage from the attack of the space locusts." He got up and went back to the chart board, where he flipped to a diagram that represented the underbelly of *Daystar*. He pointed to several areas. "As we lifted off from Mount Wildersarn, several space locusts attacked the underbelly, causing small holes in the outer hull." Thrax sat back down. "Most of the damage has been repaired, and Studs says he'll have the rest completed in a few days, but . . ." Thrax fell silent for so long that everyone stared at him.

"What's wrong, First?" Edge asked.

"Well, sir, there's a problem."

"Another problem? What kind of problem?"

"I don't know exactly. We've discovered some strange sort of liquid . . ." Thrax shrugged, his pale eyes reflecting his puzzlement. "It's coating the ship's skin around one of the holes." He turned to the medical officer. "Dr. Cole has been trying to get a handle on what the liquid is."

Temple Cole was twenty-seven years old and very attractive. Sometime in the past, the entire crew of a starship had died in a space disaster, and she had been blamed. Captain Edge and the crew believed her when she explained that her superior officer was really to blame but had made her the scapegoat. She had signed on as the *Daystar's* surgeon.

"What have you found out, Doctor?" Edge asked briskly.

"Well, all the crew seems fine," she said. "Which is a little surprising, considering the ordeal we had with those blasted space locusts."

The captain grinned impishly and reminded her, "Don't forget about Heck." Everyone chuckled again, and then Edge asked, "So what have you come up with on that substance Thrax is talking about?"

"Well, the initial findings are that the substance is very caustic, and it's acidic too. It turns into what seems to be a highly concentrated type of resin."

"Resin?" Edge's voice was tinged with surprise, and his eyes opened wide. "That would mean it's biochemical."

"That's right," Dr. Cole agreed. "But so far the computer data banks haven't identified the substance." She hesitated, then added before Edge could speak, "And there are other problems, Captain."

"What kind of problems?"

"Number one, we don't know what the substance is. Number two, we don't know what created the substance. And third, we don't know if what created it is hidden somewhere aboard the *Daystar."*

Edge suddenly exploded. "Why wasn't I told about all this before?"

"Captain, we didn't know it was biochemical," Thrax said quickly, "until just before this meeting."

Edge gripped the side of the table and allowed his anger to subside. "All right," he grumbled, "let's have the rest of the status reports. What else is wrong?"

Ivan Petroski reported that engineering was ship-shape. But he added, with a shrug, "Except there's some kind of a small power drain that we haven't been able to locate."

"What do you *mean* you can't locate it?" Edge demanded. "That's your job!"

"I've assigned Heck Jordan the task of finding it. He's usually pretty good at that sort of thing. But he hasn't been able to come up with anything yet. And it's strange, because the power drain doesn't show up in the power grids."

All the fuel cells channeled their energy through *Daystar*'s power grids. This device measured fuel cell reserves as well as power drains. When the power drained beyond a preset limit, the grid sounded an alarm. Strangely, the chief engineer said, the alarms had not been sounding.

Captain Edge puzzled over what he had just heard. He knew that Ivan had a sixth sense about some things, and the power grids were one of those. And yet, Petroski knew there was a power drain but couldn't exactly point his finger at the reason for it.

"Well . . . such power drains are normal some-times," Edge said thoughtfully. "But button it down as soon as possible, Ivan. Oh, and have Ericson assigned to help Jordan fix it. We're flying into trouble, and I don't want any power problems." He turned then to the navigator. "Bronwen, where are we, and where are we going?"

Bronwen Llewellen was an attractive older woman.

51

She had silver hair, dark blue eyes, and was famous among the space fleet as the best navigator ever turned out. She was also a Christian, perhaps the firmest believer any aboard the *Daystar* had ever seen. Bronwen spoke in a quiet voice as she gave her report.

"As you've already explained, we are heading toward the Rainbow Nebula." She pointed to the galaxy that filled the port of the conference room. "In the very center of the nebula is a black hole. As the black hole rotates, it charges the ions in the gas cloud. In a way we don't understand yet, these charges from the black hole must vary, causing the ions to light up in every spectrum of the rainbow."

Edge again thought the room felt chilly, and one could hear a pin drop.

Bronwen continued, getting up and pointing out several areas in the gas cloud. "We know that there's something in that gas cloud. We don't know exactly what, but Galactic Command believes that *something* has caused the disappearance of our ships over the years." The navigator walked back to the table as she concluded her report. "I almost disappeared in the Rainbow Nebula once myself."

"Tell us about it, Bronwen," the captain requested.

Bronwen sat down and rubbed both arms. "I was navigator aboard one of the early Explorer Class starships a few years ago. The ship was named the *Hawkins*."

"How many years ago was that?" Zeno asked.

"More years ago than I'm going to admit to publicly, Mr. First Officer," she snapped, and everybody chuckled. "Our mission was to explore the Rainbow Nebula and study the variances of its black hole as compared with other black holes."

The navigator started to tap her finger lightly on the table. "I happened to be on the bridge when my navigational beacon sounded an alarm. I checked the ship's sensor arrays—nothing registered on them. I checked weapons computers—they too did not register anything. Only my navigation computer told me *something* was in the cloud with us and that it was headed directly for us." She spoke haltingly. "For some unknown reason, God protected me from what happened next."

Edge glanced around the table. Everyone appeared to be sitting on the edge of his chair.

"What did happen next?" Ivan asked.

"Everybody aboard the *Hawkins* became hysterical."

Captain Edge asked the obvious question. "Why?"

Bronwen looked at him. "I don't understand why, Captain. Neither does Galactic Command. I don't suppose anyone does. All I do know is that, if that effect can be harnessed, it would make a dreadful weapon—especially against us."

"How did you escape?" Dr. Cole asked.

"God is really the only answer I have. When I saw the crew running around screaming as if they were being chased by invisible monsters, I secured the bridge with a special encryption code and used my navigational beacon to guide us out of the gas cloud."

Bronwen absently folded a piece of paper in half and started to crease the fold. "Just before exiting the cloud, I was visually checking the gas cloud when I saw something. It looked like a giant thread—and the gases of the nebula flowed around it as it moved in space."

"Over the years have you come to any conclusions about the thread, Bronwen?" Edge asked.

"As a matter of fact, I have. I believe the gas clouds of the Rainbow Nebula contain gravitron threads. These threads attach themselves to matter and then draw that matter into the black hole."

Ivan sat straight up in his chair. "Gravitron threads! I just read an article about them a couple of months ago. They do more than pull on matter—they distort it. Some sort of interdimensional effect is the best guess of the so-called experts. No wonder the crew went mad. These threads disrupt the cell integrity of the central nervous system."

"What happened to the crew, Bronwen?" Dr. Cole asked gently.

Bronwen made another crease in her piece of paper. "After I cleared the *Hawkins* from the Rainbow Nebula a couple of sectors, I tried to contact the captain. I received no response from him. I received no response from anyone! Internal scanners indicated that I was the only one alive out of thirty-five persons assigned to the ship!

"So I left the bridge to investigate. What I saw was horrible. Everyone had died with a look of terror on his face. I don't know what they saw, but each died scared out of his wits." Bronwen crumpled the paper in her hand. "I have no explanation as to why I survived and they didn't. The whole time, I never saw, heard, or felt anything frightening. God spared me is all I can say."

The senior officers of the *Daystar* sat stunned. Even Ivan was at a loss for words. Bronwen then reported the date and time that *Daystar* would enter the Rainbow Nebula. It was too soon for comfort.

Pushing his chair back from the table, Captain Edge said, "All right. Meeting dismissed. All available crew to scan the ship for unwelcome life-forms."

As everyone left the bridge, Edge looked out the conference port at the Rainbow Nebula and thought, *How could anything that beautiful be so dangerous and be like the Bermuda Triangle back in the twenti-eth century?* He moved his shoulders restlessly and muttered aloud as he stepped out into the corridor, "And why in the name of Jupiter is Commandant Lee ordering a crew of kids into such a dangerous part of the galaxy? I wonder if she's lost her mind."

Dr. Cole had stopped to look out a porthole.

"A good meeting?" she asked sarcastically.

"Yes, it was. Informative." He smiled at her warmly. He knew that Temple Cole was still suspicious of men. Any men. She had been in love with the man who had betrayed her, and it was difficult for her to rid herself of suspicion.

"I'm worried about what lies ahead of us, Mark."

"Never knew you to be worried before."

"Well, I don't worry about things that can be explained. But unexplainable things happen to humans in that sector. I've done some research into the Rainbow Nebula myself, and it bothers me."

"What especially bothers you?"

"For one thing, there is no *life* anywhere near it. Everywhere we've traveled, there is at least something alive, even if it's just microbes. But the Rainbow Nebula is devoid of life. I believe we're dealing with forces of nature here that nobody understands. If you ask me, the black hole in this nebula is a life drain."

"How do you mean?"

"If Bronwen is correct in her observations, the gravitron threads didn't attack the gas cloud nor did it tractor the ship toward the black hole. According to Bronwen, the only thing that was attacked was the ship's crew. I find that a fascinating distinction to be made by a phenomenon of nature."

Edge saw that his medical officer was indeed worried.

"I'd like to have a private talk with Bronwen," she said. "She knows more about this thing than any of the rest of us."

"We'll go together," he said and smiled. "I like it when we do things together."

Captain Edge had left Zeno Thrax in charge of the bridge. The Rainbow Nebula with its huge black hole filled the forward view screen, but right now the first officer was concerned about the intruder that he believed was on the ship. He hoped his expression was so blank that it was difficult for anyone to figure out his mood.

"Raina, get me Brutarius on Capella."

"Just a moment, sir. I have to filter out the interference first." Raina was adjusting her communication grids to filter out the noise-filled frequencies the Rainbow Nebula was emitting. After several minutes, she said, "I have Brutarius. I've channeled him to your screen."

Brutarius and his wife, Anmoir, were standing on a balcony that faced the Great Plain of Capella. Columns of heavy black smoke were rising into the air some distance behind them.

Suzerain Brutarius was not a tall man or muscular. He was wiry, however, and strong, and there was an air of command about him. He wore the dark green robe forbidden to all except the royal family of Capella. Anmoir was a small-boned, fair-haired woman. She also wore the royal green.

Zeno humbly greeted the royal family. "I'm very sorry, Your Majesties. This matter is very urgent, and I'm thankful you could find time for us."

Brutarius smiled broadly. "Zeno, no need for formality here. What can we help you with?"

Zeno tried to keep his face emotionless, but Brutarius and Anmoir could probably tell that something indeed urgent had prompted this communication. "Sire, we're not really sure if we have a problem or not." He settled back in the captain's chair. "You'll remember that the *Daystar* was attacked by those ugly insects while we were lifting off."

"I remember very well." Then the suzerain said, "You and the others saved our lives. A debt we can never truly repay. What is your problem?"

"We *think* we have a problem. Our crew chief has been repairing the holes made by the locusts in our outer hull. Nothing really serious, and repairs are proceeding faster than we thought." Zeno cleared his throat, because he was not used to speaking with royalty. "The problem may be nothing. But there was a coating of resin on and in one of the holes. We've also discovered that some sort of acid has eaten through into the inner hull. Then one of our crewmen reported seeing something small that was white and beige . . ."

Brutarius held up a hand, palm out toward Zeno. "Zeno, you and your crew are in danger. The animal you speak of is called a borator on our planet. They're few in number and normally live out in the wilderness areas. You'll be safe *only* as long as you watch for them and stay out of their way."

Raina said, "So they're kind of like a poisonous snake on Earth? Stay away from them, and they'll stay away from you?"

Brutarius answered, "I confess I don't know much about Earth snakes, but indeed you are all in danger. When the borator bites, it injects a caustic acid into its victim's bloodstream. Death occurs within seconds."

"Zeno, there's no antidote for this acid," Anmoir put in gravely. "One's internal organs turn into liquid almost instantly. It is a very painful death. One of them must have crawled up onto the ship when you landed on Mount Wildersarn."

"Can you give us a better description of the borator?" Zeno asked.

Brutarius scratched his blond head and thought for a moment. "It sounds like you have a young one, if its colors are still beige and white. They turn green and black when they mature. The acid is the same strength, however. The animal is small." Brutarius held up his wife's hand. "About as large as Anmoir's hand."

"Is there a way to catch it?" Zeno inquired.

"*Catching* borators is not the problem. Just prepare a mound of crystalline minerals on the deck and wait. The borator loves crystals and gemstones of all kinds."

At that moment, some men yelled in the background, and Brutarius looked to see what was going on. Then he turned back to Zeno. "I'm sorry, we have a matter to attend to. We're still rounding up the remaining locusts. For insects, they are very intelligent."

Brutarius disappeared from the viewer. Zeno could hear his deep voice as he gave his men orders.

Anmoir, however, was still looking from the screen at Zeno. "The problem my husband was about to tell you about was that there is no way to hold onto the borator once you catch it. Their acid eats through anything. So don't *try* to capture it. Use your Neuromags to destroy it the moment you see it. Believe me, for such a little creature it can cause a lot of damage in the wrong place. And the *Daystar* is definitely the wrong place!" Queen Anmoir's face disappeared from the screen.

Zeno had a lot he needed to share with Captain Edge. He was just about to summon him when the bridge alarm sounded.

"Raina, what's the alarm going off for?"

Raina checked her alarm monitors, then said, "Mr. Thrax, someone is trying to break into the ship's secured vault!"

"Zeno to Cagney."

"Cagney here."

"Send an armed team to the security vault."

"We're already on our way."

"I'll meet you there," Zeno responded. He ran to the Neuromag locker and drew out two weapons. He handed a Neuromag to Raina, saying, "Just in case," and left her in charge of the bridge until he returned.

When Zeno Thrax arrived at the secured vault, the security team was already there. Putrid smoke filled the air. It was enough to make anyone nauseated. Cagney was kneeling in front of the force field that surrounded the vault. The opaque force field was still in place.

"Mr. Thrax, there's a hole in the floor here that is a twin to the one we found on the outer hull." He started to stick his finger into the hole.

"Don't touch it!" Zeno warned and pulled the chief away.

Captain Edge had arrived just in time to see this.

"What's going on, First?" he asked sternly.

Zeno quickly reported everything that Brutarius and Anmoir had told him earlier.

Then Captain Edge examined the small hole without touching it.

"Apparently, our little friend could smell the tridium crystals in the vault and decided he would have some lunch—except that the force field must have soured his appetite a little."

The captain was not in a good humor. He would

prefer to have a saboteur that was man-sized rather than this little borator animal. He turned to Zeno Thrax. "Zeno, I want you to issue Neuromags to everyone on board. Beef up the security shields protecting the vital parts of the ship."

The captain then looked at Studs Cagney. "Studs, you get the grunts on this right away. I want this animal found and terminated as soon as possible. I won't sacrifice a single human life. I'll get Cole working on a possible antidote."

As Edge left the secured vault area, he could hear Cagney barking orders at the grunts.

7

The Only Answer

Bronwen Llewellen sat upright in front of the navigation console. The navigator had brought in special equipment that might help her detect the gravitron threads much earlier. Since little was known about them, she was brainstorming for every contingency she could think of. Several devices were stacked on top of the console.

One by one, Bronwen connected the individual components so that they interfaced with the main navigational computer. When the hookups were completed, the navigational console looked like an electronic Christmas tree. Multicolored lights flashed everywhere. Her next project was the star charts.

As the silver-haired woman manipulated the charts before her, a thought that had been plaguing her severely came to mind again: *Why would Commandant Winona Lee send us to such a perilous area?*

Her mind went back to the incident that was etched forever on her memory—her prior journey to the Rainbow Nebula. *Why was I kept alive?* she asked herself silently. *Why was I so special? When I get to heaven, this will be one of my first questions.*

Then she shrugged her trim shoulders and focused on the screen before her. She had already fixed in her mind the measurements of the Rainbow Nebula. The nebula measured 4.25 light-years in diameter—the same distance as from Earth's sun to Proxima Centauri, the nearest star to Earth's solar system. She thought about the gravitronic threads that interacted with each other, causing the ion particles in the nebula to change colors constantly. And another question entered her mind. *How does that happen?* In any event, the effect was dazzling, hence the name *Rainbow Nebula.*

Hearing familiar footsteps, Bronwen turned to see Jerusha entering the navigation area. "Hello, Jerusha. Have a seat." She had always liked the girl and had sensed lately that something was troubling her.

"What are you working on, Bronwen?"

"Jerusha, you're the engineering genius around here—you tell *me*."

Jerusha stood back from the navigation console and assessed the equipment that Bronwen had installed. She pointed to the different devices. "This measures bio-electrical impulses. These two devices are bidirectional ion converters. This last one is very interesting. I think it's a spectral converter, but it looks like it has been piggybacked on an enhanced frequency modulator."

"You're pretty good, young lady!"

"I know the devices, but how are you programming their use in the navigational computer?"

Bronwen adjusted a couple of switches. "If the gravitron threads head our direction, I want to be able to steer *Daystar* away from them. I've never done this before, but it will have to do. We need to pray for the Lord's help. The last thing we need is to go crazy while we're being chased by who knows what forces."

"But from what you said, I thought the crew of the *Hawkins* became hysterical and their own fears killed them," Jerusha said as she examined the different settings Bronwen was using.

"Unfortunately, when weird things happen to a person's mind, insanity is one of the few things non-Christians will accept for an explanation. What happened aboard the *Hawkins* might not ever be understood, but our scientists love to name everything. It makes them feel better. Insanity they called it, and I didn't argue with them."

Bronwen's eyes became suddenly teary. "When I was assigned to the *Hawkins*, my daily prayer was that the Lord would reveal Himself on the ship in a powerful way. To my knowledge, I was the only Christian aboard. We had a shipful of scientific experts, and not one of them knew Jesus." She pointed to a green switch. "Could you turn that switch up by fifteen percent?"

Jerusha made the adjustment, then worked with Bronwen on the navigation console for more than an hour. She seemed to be listening intently to everything the navigator had to say. But as soon as Bronwen finished, she asked, "Bronwen, what do you think about Sanara and the royal family?"

The question surprised Bronwen. She lifted her eyebrows and said, "Why, since the whole royal family became Christians, I foresee a bright future for the planet Capella. There'll be problems, of course, but it's going to be a lot different there. Christians always make a difference." She started to preach on her favorite subject. "Without God, people lose their ability to discern between right and wrong. We should never place our feelings and opinions above God's Word . . ."

Then Bronwen realized that she had hopped up onto her soapbox and hadn't noticed the hurt in Jerusha's face. "What's wrong, Jerusha? I know something's troubling you."

Jerusha did not answer for a while, and then she asked a question that seemed an evasion. "Bronwen, what was your childhood like?"

Bronwen was surprised by this question, too, but she began speaking of her childhood.

"I suppose I had the best childhood that anyone could have. There was a lot of love in my family. Dai's father was my brother—Dee."

"Dee Bando! I've heard of him," Jerusha realized.

"He inherited our father's sense of adventure as well as his brains. Dee thought he could do anything." She smiled as she thought of him. "We were the best of friends—mainly because I let him win at everything. Seeing him so happy meant more to me than winning myself."

"I know he died, Bronwen. You've never told anyone aboard *Daystar* how he died. Dai has never mentioned it, either."

"I promise to tell you that story someday, but not today. We're talking about *you* and not *me*, young lady!" She brought the conversation back to Jerusha. "Why are you asking me about my childhood, Jerusha?"

"It's just that—" Jerusha hesitated and bit her lower lip. She appeared uncomfortable and moved uneasily in her chair. For a time she seemed to struggle as to what to say. "I . . . I guess I might as well admit that I've been somewhat jealous of Sanara."

"Why should you be jealous of her?"

"It's just that she's got everything. She's beautiful, and she's a princess—but most of all, she's had a family all of her life. I don't really envy her beauty, and I wouldn't want to be in a royal family, but, Bronwen, I never had any family at all to speak of. And somehow it seems I've been . . . well . . . *cheated,* you might say."

Bronwen listened carefully as Jerusha talked on. The older woman had the gift of listening well, and she also had a deep fund of wisdom over long years of living and encountering all kinds of problems. Now, as she looked into the girl's troubled eyes, she said very thoughtfully, "The trouble you're having, Jerusha, really doesn't have anything to do with the royal family. They don't deserve all the bad thoughts you've been having about them. The real problem," she added gently, "is your own heart."

"I know that!" Jerusha said defensively. "Well, maybe I didn't always know it, but I'm just so confused, and I can't get the best of these emotions."

Bronwen ran her fingers through her hair and prayed quietly for the words of counsel that this girl so desperately needed. Finally she said, "Jerusha, all people have conflicts in their lives. There are no exceptions. If you would go to Brutarius and his wife and Sanara, you would find that they have difficulties, too. And all these issues have to be dealt with by the Holy Spirit."

"But I prayed that God would help me."

"I know you have, dear, but the Holy Spirit deals with these problems in His own timing. I think right now that it's His time to bring healing to the part of your heart that is so fragmented and troubled and confused. You know, sometimes this healing process involves walking through some pain. You will remember that Jesus suffered every temptation we did."

"I can't believe He was envious or jealous!"

"I don't understand, either, how the Son of God could have had some of the temptations that I've had, but the Scripture says that somehow it's so."

"But what can I do, Bronwen?"

"I wish I had a quick answer, an easy way, but there isn't one. It's the same for every problem, the same for every person. It sounds almost trite to say it, but what you must do is seek the Lord Himself, and this you already know. He's the answer to every one of our problems."

Jerusha sat quietly as Bronwen began to quote Scripture to encourage her. At last she got up, saying shortly, "Thanks for your time, Bronwen. It's always good to talk to you."

At the very moment she spoke those words, her eyes fell upon the screen. She pointed to a tiny blipping object inside the Rainbow Nebula. "What's that, Bronwen?"

Bronwen had taken her eyes off the screen, but she looked back to where Jerusha was pointing. Quickly she started manipulating switches. However, because of interference from the Rainbow Nebula itself, she couldn't be certain what they were seeing.

Jerusha apparently assumed that, whatever it was, it was minor. She turned away and said, "I wish my mind was full of pleasant childhood memories instead of the ones I've got."

Bronwen did not take her eyes off the screen, but she said quickly, "One of the hardest things for me to do is to point out to a close friend a fault in her character."

"You mean mine?"

"Yes. I think you're suffering from what's usually called *self-pity*, Jerusha."

Jerusha stiffened. "I didn't think you'd say that to me, Bronwen!"

"Don't be surprised by the self-pitying. It comes to all of us. I don't think there's a man or a woman or a young person on earth who hasn't allowed self-pity to come to them. But it's destructive, Jerusha. Feeling sorry for yourself is exactly what the dark powers would like most, for you are no good to God when you are wallowing in self-pity. But I'll pray for you that you'll find your way out of this trouble. I know God is able."

The navigator never took her eyes off the star charts, but she heard Jerusha's footsteps as the girl left, and she wondered, *Lord, did I do the right thing? Was I kind? Did I give her the right counsel?* It always troubled Bronwen when there was not a response on the part of those she counseled. She knew she would be up late tonight, praying for this girl.

Now, however, she rapidly manipulated the control switches in front of her, muttering, "I've got to find out what that object is. If it's a spaceship, it has no idea of the danger it's in!"

8

Tara Jaleel's Threat

Tara Jaleel was putting the final touches on the workout room. She was, in fact, converting the exercise area into a Shiva shrine. Exotic statues, wall hangings, and pictures adorned every wall. At one end of the room stood a ten-foot statue of the goddess. Shiva had six arms that were outstretched so that her hands held up a giant golden ring. She was the goddess of love and war. She was hideous.

But Tara Jaleel worshiped Shiva and talked to the statue just as if it were alive. "Help me to be more like you," she prayed aloud. "Shiva, I have come a long way in learning the art of Jain Jayati. My fighting abilities are at your service, and I most humbly thank you for your guidance. But, if I may, I ask you to reveal to me all truth. I have made little progress in developing love. I fully know how to fight, and I know how to hate. Help me to know love as well as war. Fill me with all truth so that I may be your loyal follower."

Then Tara bowed low before the statue and left the room.

As usual, as soon as Dai Bando and Heck Jordan stepped into the training room, Heck began acting nervous. "I just hope Tara Jaleel doesn't show up."

"I don't think she will," Dai said easily. "She never does at this time of day. OK, let's just do some warm-ups. First of all, maybe just some bending exercises."

They both were wearing loose-fitting white trousers and jackets for ease in exercising.

Dai bent over and put the palms of his hands flat on the floor.

Heck could barely touch his knees.

But Dai did not criticize. Instead, he said, "That's good. Just a few stretches."

Soon, however, Heck was gasping. "Isn't that about enough of these? I'm about stretched out."

"Sure. Now we'll do some light work on the weights. Nothing very serious."

The two went over to the universal weight machines, and Dai set his to bench press three hundred pounds. He lifted it as easily if it were made of foam. Beside him, Heck was soon huffing and puffing and straining with fifty pounds.

The boys worked out for a while, and, to Dai's surprise, Heck complained less than he had expected. "You're doing great, Heck," Dai told him. "If you just keep this up for a few months, you'll be a new man."

Heck made a face and wiped the sweat from his forehead with his sleeve. Then he gave Dai a closer look. "What's the matter with you today, Dai?"

"Why, nothing. What makes you ask that?"

"You look . . . funny," he said. "Are you worried about something?"

Dai stood looking around the weapons officer's exercise room. "Well, to be truthful, Heck, I don't like what Lieutenant Jaleel has done to this room."

"Really? It looks cool to me!" Heck glanced at the statue of Shiva and said, "I think that's a pretty neat piece of work."

Dai knew, of course, that Heck had no spiritual discernment whatsoever. He also knew that it would be useless to try to explain the dangers that could come from having the dark influence of idols around. Instead, he began to work with Heck on a program that he had designed to bring the boy back to a reasonable weight.

This time Heck began to complain almost at once. He was right in the middle of a complaint when Tara Jaleel came through the door. She also was wearing a loose white uniform.

The weapons officer was a Masai woman, a descendant of one of the fiercest tribes of Earth's Africa back in the twentieth century. She was twenty-four years old, was at least six feet tall, and her features were fierce, though attractive. She loved battle of any sort, as her ancestors had, and she made life miserable for everyone who had to undergo the strict training that she put them through.

"Well, Jordan, did you decide to get some of that lard off of you?"

Heck grinned weakly. "I thought I might try a little, Lieutenant."

"Heck and I decided to work out regularly," Dai said quickly. "I knew you would be in favor of that."

Dai's words brought the dark eyes of the Masai officer to fix on him, but she did not respond to his comment.

Jaleel had no liking for anybody on the spaceship, it seemed, but her special vindictiveness was focused on Dai Bando. He was aware of that. Dai was the only person she had ever encountered whom she could not conquer with her martial skills. It appeared to infuriate her even more that, although it was obvious he could have defeated her easily, he never did. He simply avoided her blows. He just seemed to float around, making it literally impossible for her to make contact.

For some time Dai took Heck through his exercises, Dai easily and Heck puffing and blowing, while Tara Jaleel stood watching. Then a movement caught Dai's eye, and Jerusha and Contessa came through the door.

"Hello, Jerusha," Dai called. "You want to join us?"

The blonde ensign frowned slightly. "No. I'll do my own thing," she said rather shortly. Then she glanced around the room and, like Dai, apparently did not like what she saw.

Heck, during the next break, must have decided that he would impress Jerusha. He swaggered over to where Contessa stood and patted the dog on the head. Actually she liked him, for he sometimes slipped her bits of candy when no one was looking.

"Hey, Jerusha," he said, "look at this. I'm getting stronger every day. I can even pick up Contessa now."

"I wouldn't try that!" Jerusha said with alarm. Everybody knew that the big German shepherd did not like to be handled.

Her warning was useless, however, for Heck stooped, put his arms about the dog, and then straightened up.

It was a disaster! The massive weight of the huge dog threw Heck off balance. He staggered backward, fell full length, and struck his head against the bulkhead. If it had not been padded, he would probably have scrambled his brains. As it was, he lay stretched out flat. Contessa sat on his stomach and licked his face.

Jerusha and Dai hurried over.

"Are you all right, Heck?" she asked worriedly.

Heck crawled to his feet and rubbed the back of his head. "I'm all right. I'm fine. What makes you think I'm not? I did that on purpose."

Tara Jaleel snorted with impatience. "On purpose! You couldn't pick up a puppy!" She ran to Heck then, seized him from behind, and was about to throw him across the room.

At that moment, however, Contessa leaped. Her solid body rammed against Tara Jaleel and forced her to loose her hold on Heck.

Jaleel's anger exploded, and she screamed, "I'm going to throw that dog out the airlock!"

Contessa stood alert, her lips drawn back from her enormous teeth, awaiting Jaleel's attack. Dai and Jerusha ran to the dog and held her.

Tara continued to breathe out threats and warnings but finally walked out, saying, "Say good-bye to that dog! I'm getting rid of her!"

Dai turned to Jerusha. "You'd better keep a close watch on Contessa. I don't like to talk about our officers, but Tara Jaleel might do exactly what she says."

Jerusha knelt and put her arms around her dog. "What would I do without you, girl?" she whispered.

Dai watched the girl, and his heart went out to her. He had learned to admire and respect Jerusha a great deal, and he loved the dog, himself. "Don't worry, Jerusha. We'll all keep an eye on Contessa. We'll put the word out to the other Rangers too. Won't we, Heck?"

"Sure we will. And if Tara Jaleel gives you any trouble, Jerusha, let me know," Heck blustered. "I'll settle her uppity attitude fast."

Dai could not help smiling, and neither could Jerusha. They both knew that Heck was terrified of the weapons officer. But Dai said, "That's good, Heck. We'll depend on you to do that."

Temple Cole rested her back against the bulkhead and glanced around the sickbay. She was weary for she had put in long hours trying to analyze that resinlike material found on *Daystar*'s underbelly. Most resins were the product of different kinds of plant life. She knew that. But this resin resembled none of those. This sample appeared to be acidic in its fluid state and then quickly dried into solidified resin, almost like a biological epoxy coating. Dr. Cole had never seen anything like it and had been unable to find any data explaining this process.

"Captain, this resin is definitely of biological origin."

"Not much doubt about that if it's from a borator," Edge concluded.

"I don't know—I have absolutely no idea—what kind of animal it came from. There's something else here that bothers me a great deal. Come and take a look."

Edge moved to her side and looked through her microscope. What he saw was a complex of honey-combed patterns, resembling a beehive except much smaller.

"What we have here," she said, "is a rare chemical complex. It's very dangerous to vertebrates."

"You mean to humans, even?"

"*Especially* to humans. This acid can burn through any of the ship's titanium hybrid metals, glass, plastics, anything! And if anybody aboard the *Daystar* is bitten, he will die almost instantly."

A worried look swept across Captain Edge's face. "Can you prepare an antidote for it?"

"I'm already working on that, Captain. I'll do the best I can, but I'm just not hopeful."

He frowned. "I was afraid you'd say that." Then he looked at his chronometer. "Well, I need to get with Ivan and check out the progress he's making on the repairs—and that power drain."

A swift burst of anger erupted from Captain Edge, and he smacked his fist into his left hand. "Something funny's going on around here, Temple, and I'm going to find out what it is!" He whirled to leave, spitting out the words, "Contact me as soon as you make progress with the antidote."

Once out in the main corridor, he switched on the ship's communication system and began to speak rapidly. "Attention, all hands! Be on the alert for a dangerous creature. *Anything* that looks unusual, report at once. Do not—I repeat do *not*—make any contact with this alien life-form. It could mean your life!"

9

Heck Buys Some Time

Ivan Petroski resembled a thermometer. He had a face as red as the glow that said "hot." It was not unusual for Petroski to lose his temper, but this time both Jerusha and Heck, who stood before him, knew that this was a temper tantrum to set off the seismographs back on Earth.

Petroski stood in the center of his domain, the Engineering sector, where the power grids were located. The large flow boards helped the chief engineer to check fuel quantity, fuel usage, and fuel reserves. Anytime the fuel cells were called upon for energy, the fuel chart measured the amount used and what it was used for. Anytime the fuel quantity lowered, there must have been a direct correlation with fuel consumption. Starships could not operate indefinitely without recharging their fuel cells.

"As you both can plainly see, more energy is being used than the chart indicates we have used. There's a power drain somewhere, and I want it found!" Ivan hit the wall with his fist. "I don't know what's going on around here," he shouted, "but I'm going to get to the bottom of it if I have to turn everybody on this ship wrong side out!"

Heck had a sinking sensation, knowing that he was the guilty party. But he put an innocent expression on his face and said in a hurt tone, "I don't know why you're picking on us, Chief."

"I'm picking on you because you two are part of

the Engineering crew! And when something goes wrong, somebody in Engineering is responsible!" Petroski peered through narrowed eyes at the chubby Space Ranger. "If I had to make a guess, I'd say it's *you*, Jordan. You're at the bottom of most things that go wrong on this cruiser."

"How can you say that, Chief? Why, I do my work as well as anybody on this ship."

"And you also get into more trouble than anybody on this ship."

"Just a minute, Chief," Jerusha put in quickly. She was biting her lower lip. "It may be just a malfunction of something mechanical. Maybe *none* of the crew is responsible."

This suggestion merely inflamed Petroski's temper. It was like throwing gasoline on an open fire. "Mechanical failure!" he shouted, jumping up and down. "*Mechanical failure!* I'll have you know the *Daystar* is in perfect condition! I could keep this ship running as smooth as any ship in space if I didn't have a bunch of nursery babies to take care of! I said all the time that Captain Edge was making a mistake when he allowed you babies to come on board, and now I know it!"

"What exactly do you think is happening here?" Jerusha asked soothingly, obviously trying to calm down the small man.

"I don't know what's happening! That's what I'm telling you. Every time I think I detect the source of the power drain, it just vanishes—like a rabbit down a hole! And then later it pops up again."

"But how do you explain that, Chief?" Heck said innocently.

Glaring at him, Ivan Petroski said, "I told you I don't know! I'm about to the point where I believe that this power grid has got a mind of its own and is working against me."

"Well, it's certain that can't be true," Jerusha ventured. "No matter how sophisticated a power grid computer is, it's still just a dumb machine. It doesn't have a mind of its own."

"I *know* that, but that's what it seems like!" Petroski shot back.

"Look, Chief," she said quietly, "you've worked on this too long. You know how it is when you get a hard problem and you work on it until your mind goes numb. Why don't you take a break? Go get some melon nectar, read a book, take a nap. Why, the answer might just pop right into your mind when you're rested. In the meantime, Heck and I will stay here and see what we can figure out."

For a moment Petroski looked ready to veto Jerusha's suggestion, but he was clearly feeling frustration from his failure to locate the power loss. "All right, all right," he said grumpily, "but you two better do something, or I'll make it rough on both of you!"

As the chief stormed out, Heck chuckled and slapped his thigh. "That little squirt. He's about as much of a chief engineer as I am a dolphin."

Jerusha turned on him, and her eyes narrowed. Her lips drew into a tight line, and taking a deep breath she said sternly, "All right, Heck. What's this all about?"

"All about? Why are you asking me?"

"Because I know that Petroski's right. You're at the bottom of this—one way or other."

"Everybody always blames me!"

"And that's because you're usually guilty. Now, you tell me what's going on."

Heck attempted to put an innocent expression on his face. Then he reached into his pocket, pulled out a package of chocolate-covered mints, and popped half a dozen of them into his mouth. As he chewed on them, he muttered, "I don't know why you think it's me. It could be anybody else. Maybe just a mechanical problem. This ship's not perfect. No matter what Petroski says."

"Now, Heck, you listen to me," Jerusha said. "There are only four people on board this cruiser who are capable of diverting energy from the power grid. There's Captain Edge, Petroski, myself, and then there's you. I know it's not the first three, so by process of deduction it has to be *you*."

Heck felt his face grow rosy as Jerusha continued to pound at him with her voice. He kept on stuffing chocolate-covered mints into his mouth, though, all the time protesting his innocence. He also kept glancing at the power grid.

Finally Jerusha said, "Heck, you could easily monitor the power grids and know when Ivan was checking on the power drain. The question here is *why*. What do you need the power for, big guy?"

Suddenly Heck saw that he was in severe danger of being exposed. *The best tactic when you're getting put down is to attack!* he thought. Swallowing a mouthful of mints, he glared at Jerusha, then said, "Who are you to be telling me what to do? Everybody knows you're going around feeling sorry for yourself. Why don't you take your big mangy dog and yourself and just leave *Daystar?* Nobody needs you here. Go off and pout somewhere else. Everybody would be a lot better off without you!"

Jerusha blinked at the attack. She opened her mouth to speak but nothing came out. Without a word she closed her lips, whirled, and marched out of Engineering, her back stiff and her fists clenched.

"Well," Heck gloated, pulling out a large chunk of fudge and biting off a wedge. "At least I'm safe for a while. It pays to know how to buy yourself a little time."

The bridge of the *Daystar* was impressive. Modern and spacious, it was rectangular in design instead of oval and allowed for three main view screens. The largest, the center screen, featured the main view. The screen to the right of the main viewer was designed for weapons and tactical. The screen on the left provided navigational information.

One large center console was positioned halfway between the captain's station and the forward view screens. This console was used by the helmsman, the navigator, and the weapons officers.

The captain's station, located at the rear center of the bridge, gave the captain a good vantage point for monitoring his bridge crew and all three screens.

Standing at the center console, Captain Edge was studying the face of Commandant Winona Lee. He had the utmost respect for the leader of the Intergalactic Space Fleet, for he knew she had a mind like a steel trap. Apparently she never forgot anything (although there were a few things in his own past that Edge would have liked her to forget).

"Captain Edge," Commandant Lee was saying firmly, "an Intergalactic Magnum Deep Space Cruiser by the name of *Wellington* has wandered into the vicinity of the Rainbow Nebula, and all communications with the ship have been lost."

"Why did they go even close to that thing, Commandant?"

"Sorry, Mark. That information is classified. Your assignment is to take the *Daystar* and investigate the whereabouts of *Wellington*, determine their present status, and render help if possible."

"Anything else, Commandant?"

"Yes," she said emphatically. "Under no circumstances endanger the *Daystar* and her crew. You have a tendency, Captain, to go galloping to the rescue of maidens in distress. I'll have none of that this time."

"Why, I don't know why you'd say that. I just—"

"Never mind the explanations, Captain Edge. This is a direct order. Do not risk your ship. Is that clear?"

"Yes, Commandant."

"Very well, then. The *Cromwell* was dispatched to the area, but it will be several days before she enters that sector of space. Time is short. I will expect your report as soon as you have one to make. Over and out."

As Commandant Lee's face faded from the viewer, Captain Edge turned to Bronwen Llewellen, who was standing by her console. "Begin scanning for the *Wellington*, Bronwen."

"I've already computed a possible location of the ship, sir."

"In your head? Well, that's probably better than the machinery we've got."

Ignoring his compliment, the navigator shifted the main view screen so that they were looking at a very small section of the Rainbow Nebula. She pointed to a shimmering white shape and said, "The problem is that the *Wellington* is getting dangerously close to the gravitron threads of the nebula's black hole."

Edge shook his head. "It sounds like a bad scene to me, Bronwen."

"Indeed. I'm afraid it may be already too late to save the ship and her crew."

It was a hard moment for Captain Edge. As a captain, he hated to see any ship lost, especially a Magnum

Deep Space Cruiser and her large crew. He thought hard, trying to think of some way, any way, to reach the ship and save them. He turned again to Bronwen. "Is there anything you see that we can do to save the *Wellington?* Surely they must have known the danger they were in!"

Bronwen Llewellen took a deep breath. "In brief answer to that, no. Captain, as you know already, it was unprecedented that I remained alive after seeing what I did in this nebula. Our science knows nothing about the power of gravitron threads. We barely know anything about black holes!"

She adjusted a couple of switches on the console as she continued. "Why would nature *need* a gravity well so strong that even light cannot escape from it? All we have are questions. The best answers we have are guesses. The ship has not been built that can withstand the crushing force generated by a black hole. In my opinion, maybe black holes have something to do with the *balance* of things."

Captain Edge switched the main viewer so that it displayed the entire Rainbow Nebula. At its center lay the black hole, which pulled into itself streams of matter turned to energy. Around the perimeter of the black hole, the gaseous nebula turned different colors of the rainbow. "What leads you to think that, Navigator?"

Bronwen looked at the main view screen. "We know there are billions of stars in just our own galaxy. Scientists believe that there are billions of galaxies! So we have billions of galaxies that contain multiple billions of stars, and each one of those stars emits vast amounts of energy." She looked down at the floor and then said thoughtfully, "It's just a guess on my part, but maybe God created the black holes to absorb energy in order to keep the whole universe in balance? Sort of like a drain in a bathtub that keeps the water from overflowing the tub? Without black holes, perhaps the universe would just heat up with energy uncontrollably. As I say, they may provide *balance*." Then Bronwen asked abruptly, "Who commands the *Wellington?*"

At the same moment something came into Edge's mind. It was a matter he had almost forgotten. He said slowly, "Toland Murphy."

His words brought Bronwen's head around. "Wasn't he the captain that Temple had on her last assignment?"

"Yes." Edge's jaw grew tense. "He captained the *Kennedy*, a medium-sized 'J' Class star cruiser. Dr. Cole was the chief medical officer. A terrible disaster occurred when one of the crewmen returned from R and R on the planet Netan. Unknowingly, the crewman was infected with the highly contagious Ebolithrax virus." Captain Edge looked away from the viewer toward Bronwen. "Before anyone knew what was happening, the virus spread through the *Kennedy* like wildfire. Dr. Cole ordered Captain Murphy to flush the ventilation system into space, because it was contaminated with the airborne virus."

Edge locked his hands behind his back. "Instead of ventilating the ship, though, he mistakenly back flushed the ship with the contaminated air. Almost the entire crew died as a result—close to three hundred people. Of course, there was an investigation. Captain Murphy told them that Dr. Cole had ordered the ventilation system flushed but not into space. Murphy won his case, and Temple lost her medical license. It's a miracle that she didn't wind up in prison the rest of her life."

"So the reappearance of Captain Murphy is not going to be good news for Temple, then," Bronwen said.

"I'm afraid not. It's an ugly chapter of her past turning up. And none of us likes to see a ghost from the past—or three hundred ghosts—suddenly at our doorstep."

Contessa and Jerusha were making their way down the main corridor toward Engineering when, quick as lightning, a small beige-and-white creature suddenly shot down the walkway in front of them. As Jerusha was trying to draw her Neuromag, Contessa broke free and raced to catch the ugly little animal.

Jerusha yelled, "Contessa, stop!"

The dog ignored her and pursued the thing until it disappeared down a floor chute.

Jerusha ran up to her big German shepherd. "You know better than that, Contessa! When I command you to stop, you *stop*."

Contessa stood sniffing at the floor chute. She started to scratch at the grill.

"That thing, whatever it is, can kill you in an instant. Leave it alone!" Jerusha knelt by the dog and seized her head. "Leave it alone, Contessa! *Leave it alone!*"

The dog stopped scratching and looked back at Jerusha. Contessa clearly had no intention of leaving it alone. It was dead meat as far as she was concerned. For the moment, though, she wagged her tail and ran on down the corridor, looking for Heck Jordan. It was time for a snack.

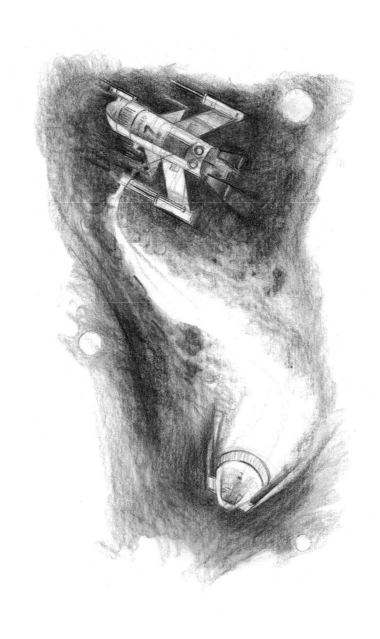

10
Gravitron Threads

Sitting in his command chair aboard the *Wellington*, Capt. Toland Murphy was about to make a final log entry on the emergency communications beacon. No other form of communication was available, for the mighty ship's antennae arrays had been destroyed.

The first thing anyone usually noticed about Captain Murphy was his long silver hair. Many people had commented that it was the youthful Murphy's best feature. He combed it straight back, and it drifted in the air like gossamer. His tan skin and blue-gray eyes accentuated his handsome face. At five ten, he was slender though strong. But some people had discovered that fine looks can be deceiving. Temple Cole was one of them.

Normally, the bridge of the *Wellington* was staffed by fifty crewmen, twenty-four hours a day, seven days a week. Now, however, only two of the crew remained alive: Chief Engineer Brian Sandoval and the captain himself.

Captain Murphy began his final log entry:

> *Captain's log, Fourteenth Millennium, 13428-07-15-1452. Captain Toland Murphy commanding Intergalactic Command Magnum Deep Space Cruiser, Wellington. Class AAA-01 encryption code 3x-457.*
>
> *For Emergency Communications Beacon.*
> *Our mission to the Rainbow Galaxy was necessitated by recent classified information con-*

cerning the Denebians. Reports indicated that the Denebians had developed a means for harnessing the power of a gravitron thread from the Rainbow Galaxy. The Denebians plan to install this weapon on all their star cruisers. Intergalactic Command interprets this action as a prelude to war and has no defense against this weapon.

Commandant Winona Lee ordered the Wellington to procure a sample of the gravitron threads. Our efforts thus far have been disastrous. One of the threads brushed the edge of the ship's stern on the aft portion of Engineering. Our fuel cells were ruptured, and our engines have suffered catastrophic damage. One of the severed star engines struck our communications antennae array—it was completely destroyed. This event cost us more than half of our crew.

As for the rest of our crew, they soon started suffering from mass hysteria, probably bordering on insanity. All are dead except for myself and my chief engineer. So far, the chief has not been affected. I am starting to feel the same effects as the crew did. It is taking all my effort to keep my feeling of hysteria in check. We have secured ourselves on the bridge.

For future reference, data indicates that crew members were seeing things that weren't there. I've scanned the ship for alien life-forms, but nothing appears on the scans other than the crew. The different crewmen I've seen die have had expressions of sheer terror on their faces. Whatever is affecting us induces uncontrollable fear.

My last report from Intergalactic Command stated that they have dispatched the Cromwell.

I'm afraid their help will be too late. Navigational sensors indicate that a gravitron thread will pass through midship shortly.

In summary, all but one of my crew are dead. Ship's power reserves are almost exhausted. Total ship's destruction will occur within the hour. For future missions to the Rainbow Nebula, my recommendation is enhancement of the navigational arrays—standard scanners do not, I repeat, do not, pick up most of the threads —and the formulation of special shielding to protect the mental health of the crew.

Captain Toland Murphy, Commanding, Wellington.

With a nod of his head, Murphy ordered Sandoval to eject the beacon into space.

Chief Engineer Brian Sandoval had the rugged features of a man who had descended from Mexican and Navajo stock. His skin was dark tan with a red tint. His hair was straight with a slight wave. It was medium length and jet black. He was slightly barrel-chested and had arms that looked as if they could bend steel.

His parents were jewelers and had hoped their only son would follow in their footsteps. To their dismay, Brian's goal was to journey into the vastness of space. Sparkling gems didn't interest him—sparkling stars did!

His grandmother had been full-blooded Navajo. Her name was Song Eyes. When he was a young lad, she used to sit with him on the front porch of their New Mexico home. They would look at the stars and then at the cacti that dotted the range. The huge plants were of every shape and had been designed to survive in the dryness of the desert. She would tell him of the ancient Navajo chiefs who lived when the prairies and mountains were wild and free. Then she would tell Brian of her love for Jesus and how He was the Chief of all chiefs.

Some nights, Song Eyes would read from the Bible and sing songs right from its pages. She helped Brian discover the truth of the universe. And under those very stars, Brian Sandoval became a believer in Jesus Christ.

Before Song Eyes died, she gave him her worn Bible.

Brian was standing at the communications console. As soon as Captain Murphy finished his message, Sandoval turned three switches, which sent the emergency communications beacon speeding from the *Wellington* toward Earth. Any Intergalactic Command vessel that picked up its distress signal would relay Captain Murphy's log entry to Earth on space communication channels that were several times the speed of light.

"Captain, we've done all that we can do," Sandoval said as he watched the beacon race away from the star cruiser. Then he turned back to the captain and continued, "Except pray, of course."

Captain Murphy looked at him as if he were seeing his chief engineer for the first time. "I didn't have any idea you were one of those Jesus people."

Brian was puzzled by that comment, but he said, "There don't seem to be many of us left—especially in Intergalactic Command."

"We've been together on *Wellington* since she was commissioned. I've never seen you at church, or praying, or anything."

Brian was more puzzled but said nothing this time.

The captain slumped back into his chair. "Sandoval, I think the gravitron effect has gotten to you.

Something must be happening to your mind. Do you see anything?"

"No, I don't see anything. I *am* starting to feel a certain anxiousness, though. I have no idea why I'm not affected like the rest of the crew. By rights we both should be dead, too, you know."

The captain sat upright. "Well, whatever the reason, I'm thankful I'm not dead. Yet." Murphy squinted several times and then rubbed his eyes. "I've never believed in ghosts, or spirits, or any sort of nightmarish hobgoblins. So I think I'm finally going crazy. Every few minutes, some fiendish-looking *thing* just appears in front of me and then disappears."

Sandoval had no idea how much longer Captain Murphy could retain his mental stability. If Brian was going to be a witness for Jesus, now was the time.

"Captain, you may not remember, but I have mentioned Jesus to you several times over the years."

"I'm sorry, but I don't remember a single time."

"I'm afraid my words fell on deaf ears. For some reason, when I tried to talk to you about God, you would immediately change the topic. If I said the word 'Jesus,' you'd walk away, telling me that you just remembered something you were supposed to do. It was as if you didn't even hear me. After a while, I just gave up and said nothing. I'm really sorry about that now."

"Why should you be sorry? What difference does it make what any of us believes? When you die, you die!"

Sandoval saw the anger in his captain's eyes, but the time was short, so he continued talking. "It makes all the difference in the world. There is tremendous evil aboard this ship. I know you think I'm crazy, but I think the crew may have been seeing wicked spirits—very hideous ones at that."

"Spirits!" Murphy scoffed. "It's beyond me how my

chief engineer, a man of science, a man whose quarters are wallpapered with degrees, could believe in the existence of *spirits!*"

Suddenly an alarm sounded. Both Captain Murphy and Brian Sandoval raced to the navigational computer. What Sandoval saw terrified him. A huge complex of gravitron threads had appeared on the screen, and they were headed straight toward the *Wellington.*

On the bridge of the *Daystar,* a frowning Captain Edge studied the main view screen. "Have they responded to any of your hails, Ensign?" he asked Raina St. Clair.

"Negative, sir. According to our scans, their antenna array has been destroyed."

Just then, he saw a tiny craft rocket away from the *Wellington.*

"There goes their emergency communications beacon. Things must be desperate for them." The captain's worried frown deepened.

Zeno Thrax reported next. "Since our scanners have been enhanced by the navigational array, computer indicates that all her fuel cells have been ruptured. The resulting explosions destroyed their star engines. The destruction to the ship's stern is extensive. Scanners indicate that there are only two crewmen left alive on the whole ship."

"Only two people left on a ship that held more than seven hundred? Where *are* the two?"

"On the bridge."

The captain got to his feet. There was a time for talking and a time for action. Now was the time for action. "How much time do they have left?"

"Ship's reserve power and life support systems will be inoperative in approximately forty minutes,"

Zeno replied. "Our scanners have also picked up a gravitron thread. Our best estimate is that it will collide with *Wellington* a few minutes after that."

"Mr. Thrax, power up our engines. I want to dock with *Wellington*'s bridge in two minutes."

"Wouldn't it be better to wait for the *Cromwell?*" Zeno cautioned.

"You have your orders. I don't like it any more than you, Zeno, but we can't sit here and wait."

Thrax's pale hands danced across the helm controls. As *Daystar* raced into danger, everyone on the bridge would hold his breath.

"I'm ready to hook up the computer to the interfacing relays," Ringo told Heck as he set the supercomputer on their worktable.

Heck pointed to a shelf at the back of the pod, indicating that that would house the computer. When Ringo took the device to the shelf, he saw the interface relays laid out in order at the shelf's rear.

"Very neat arrangement, Heck. All I have to do now is plug and play." He smiled at the thought of finally being able to walk on a faraway beach with the holographic Raina. He began to make the connections.

Heck seemed to be enjoying immensely what he was doing. "Didn't we luck out when Captain Edge didn't pick us for the rescue team?" He placed another panel back into position.

"Yeah, I guess so. Jerusha was the only Ranger chosen." Ringo paused while he adjusted a hardware switch. "Actually, I'm glad that *none* of the rest of us Space Rangers were picked. Raina especially."

"Raina, Raina, Raina! You've got Raina for brains. I bet if I could see into your head, I'd see a thousand Rainas running all over the place."

Ringo laughed, but he admitted, "Heck, I think you're right. My mind is wallpapered with Raina pictures. Anyway, when I get hooked up to this machine, I plan to be walking on the beach with only one Raina. Maybe not the real one, but if you can't have the real thing, then a holographic version will do!"

Heck turned serious. "I have only a couple more things to do, and then our holographic virtual reality machine will be operational." He used his tuning adjusters to synchronize the emitters that polka-dotted the blue interior of the pod.

"How will the pod know which brain waves to transfer onto the pod?" Ringo asked. "That's what puzzles me." He assumed it was a valid question that Heck must have spent a lot of time thinking about.

"I can't be sure yet. This technology is as new as new gets. Finding those things out will take a little practice." Heck now was gathering up some of his tools. "One thing to remember—guard your thoughts and emotions. Instead of having a nice time with Raina, you could find yourself reliving a nightmare."

"I knew this thing was too good to be true!" Ringo groaned loudly.

"Would you keep *quiet*—someone will hear us." Heck closed his toolbox and stood up. "We need to try it out as soon as possible. I know Jerusha. She knows I'm responsible for the power drains. She'll be hunting all over the ship to find out what I've been doing. We were lucky she was picked for the rescue team, or she'd be standing here right now, pointing at me with that bony finger of hers! Let's sit a minute."

The boys dropped down on a nearby bench, and Heck reached into his pocket for a couple of chocolate bars. He gave one to Ringo.

Neither ensign knew that under the floor beneath

their feet a small beige-and-white creature was sniffing around, looking for a meal.

There were only twenty-four Magnum Deep Space Cruisers in the fleet. And these were not nearly enough to adequately patrol the vastness of a galaxy that was more than a hundred billion light-years across. Several more cruisers were being built, but they wouldn't be on-line for a very long time.

It was difficult for Captain Edge to imagine a more valuable piece of property than the titanic starship that lay fatally damaged in front of him. Although he loved the *Daystar*, his ship was the size of a mouse in comparison to a Magnum Deep Space Cruiser.

Wellington hung in space, but not in anything like the usual sense—a great white ship surrounded by the blackness of space with a blanket of twinkling stars in the background.

Today she hung in an atmosphere spangled with ion-charged particles that changed colors like a liquid-light orchestra. The Rainbow Nebula was aptly named. Streams of color flowed all around the perimeter of one of the blackest holes in the galaxy. The gleaming white surface of the *Wellington* easily reflected the moving colors. The ship too changed from red to yellow, then yellow to green, then green to blue. The effect on *Daystar*'s crew was almost hypnotizing.

Squeezing his eyelids until they were nearly closed, Captain Edge ordered, "Zeno, filter the colors down 50 percent." The hues on the main viewer muted to a level that eased the strain on his eyes. Edge's gaze wandered over to the black hole.

He knew that this black hole had threads of concentrated gravity that spoked millions of miles away from the heart of its center. Spiraling across the nebula, thin threads of gravitron snaked through the multi-colored gases. It was impossible for the naked eye to see one of the threads in its natural state. It was the effect the thread had on the gases that brought its presence to light.

Moving through the nebula as easily as a child waves its arms in the air, the threads sought for energy and matter to fill the great mouth of the black hole. Astroscientists had not yet discovered what happened once something was drawn into a black hole's depths. They did know one very important fact, though—nothing returned!

"Captain, docking protocols are in effect. Permission to engage docking," Zeno Thrax requested seriously. "*Wellington* power levels are minimal. We won't be able to maintain docking for long."

Captain Edge located the docking port, which was positioned on the port side of *Wellington*'s bridge. "Affirmative to engage docking," Edge responded as he looked at his chronometer. "We won't have much time, will we?" he asked Bronwen.

She looked up from her viewer. "Not much time at all, Captain—maybe none at all. These gravitron threads are almost completely invisible, even with my enhancements. I'm not exactly sure *where* they are."

Edge looked back at his navigator. For a moment each gazed deep into the other's eyes. The look was unmistakable. They had come to yet another do-or-die situation. Hope for the best, but be prepared for the worst.

"Captain to rescue team. Meet me in the docking port."

Just as Edge finished speaking over the ship's intercom, he felt the slight jerking sensation that meant *Daystar* had docked with the *Wellington*.

And he heard Bronwen whispering a prayer as he walked past her. "Don't stop" were Edge's only words as the bridge door closed.

11

Danger Approaches

Daystar's rescue team members were donning their enviro-suits in the prep room adjacent to the docking port. These suits were essential for humans who found themselves having to journey into life-threatening environmental conditions. And the rescue team had no idea which decks aboard *Wellington* contained breathable atmosphere.

In spite of Zeno Thrax's strong objections, Captain Edge had chosen Tara Jaleel and Jerusha Ericson to accompany him on the rescue mission.

"Captain, I should lead this rescue team, not you." Thrax was being noticeably more assertive with the captain.

Edge said nothing. He continued to put on his enviro-suit.

Zeno then watched Tara and Jerusha adjusting their suits. "At least let me take Jerusha's place. This mission is far too dangerous for her."

"Mr. Thrax, I've been chosen, so I'm going," Jerusha scolded while still busy tightening the fittings to her leggings. "Don't even think about replacing me."

Edge chuckled. "Mr. Thrax, I need you to command *Daystar* while I'm gone. Help Ivan get the engines ready to fire on a moment's notice." He looked up at his first officer. "You *have* to stay on board, Zeno."

While making the final adjustments to her suit, Tara Jaleel interjected, "Relax, Thrax. There's nothing aboard that ship that I can't handle."

Edge and Thrax looked at each other knowingly. They both knew that Tara was completely serious, but her stronger-than-thou statement didn't offer any comfort. Unexplainable things happened in the Rainbow Nebula. Who could prepare for them?

"Thank you, Tara," Edge responded. "Mr. Thrax, report to the bridge and carry out my orders."

Thrax glared at him briefly, then left.

And Captain Edge thought that was the closest he'd ever seen the albino come to complete rage. It told him how dangerous the first officer knew this rescue mission was going to be.

Daystar was parked at the docking port located near *Wellington*'s bridge. The air locks from both ships signaled green, indicating that the rescue party could enter the corridor next to the bridge of the Magnum Deep Space Cruiser.

Tara read her portable scanner. "Very little oxygen in this corridor. My guess is that the life support computers have been shutting down different areas of the ship that don't contain living crewmen."

Edge considered her explanation. "You're probably right, Jaleel, but the hull is breached also, and the atmosphere could just be seeping away from the ship."

Tara was trying to adjust her scanner. "This thing's useless. The ions are causing too much interference."

Edge examined the device and agreed with her. The weapons officer hung the scanner back on her belt.

"It sure is dark in here," Jerusha said. "I think I see shapes lying on the floor over there, though." She pointed to a dark mass about thirty feet away, and the rescue team started walking in that direction.

"Turn up your suit lights," Edge ordered.

Six bodies were lying face down on the deck, all in a heap where the corridor stopped at the bridge door.

"Look at the scratch marks on the door. It looks as if they were trying to claw the door open," Tara said. She reached down to turn over the body of a young woman officer, then cried out. Both Jaleel and Jerusha backed away.

Edge instantly reached for his Neuromag, but when he saw the dead officer's expression of horror, he knew why his two crewmates had jumped back. The officer's face was frozen in terror, and her hands were gnarled tight. Her uniform was torn in shreds.

"What's happened here, Tara?" he asked.

"They were clawing at each other, trying to get away from . . . something."

Edge examined the other crewmen's hands and found bits of cloth and flesh buried under their fingernails.

"Captain Edge, what could have happened to cause this?" Jerusha appeared deeply shaken.

Edge grimaced. "I don't know. And after talking with Bronwen, I don't think anyone knows. It was insanity to send a ship near this nebula." He noted the faces of the remaining five crewmen. Each face wore an identical expression of fear. "It's probably safe to assume that everyone who has died aboard this ship looks the same as these do."

"Or were blown out into space when the fuel cells ruptured," Tara added.

Jerusha stood at the door that accessed the bridge. "Captain, these controls have been encrypted. I can't gain access to the bridge."

"Stand back, Jerusha," he ordered. He drew his Neuromag and set it on its highest setting. "I'll cut through the door locks. And we don't have much time. Any air on the bridge will be gone in minutes."

At first, the locking mechanism was resistant to the energy blast from the Neuromag, but in a few moments it turned red, then slowly to bright orange, and finally to white. Then it disappeared altogether. Edge kicked open the door.

The first thing he heard was a scream.

"They're coming to get me! Help me, Sandoval! Help me!" Murphy grabbed Brian Sandoval and pushed him toward the door to the bridge.

Sandoval had already deduced that whatever fear he was feeling in small measure, the terror-stricken crew had experienced in fullness. Now Captain Murphy was desperately trying to escape by clawing at the wall farthest from the bridge door. Brian knew that the same thing that had killed the crew was now after his captain.

When the bridge door exploded open, Sandoval thought that he too had finally been mentally affected by the Rainbow Nebula. He stood firm, though, ready to meet whatever was going to come through the shattered door.

But instead of a horde of terrifying creatures rushing through the doorway, he saw three intergalactic enviro-suits. His "Praise the Lord!" echoed across the bridge.

Tension ran high on the bridge of the *Daystar*. Raina St. Clair, Bronwen Llewellen, and Ivan Petroski had their eyes fixed on the instruments and the monitors as the rescue team went into action. Ivan was so edgy that he tore himself away from the monitor in front of him, paced about nervously, and pulled on his hair.

"Will you settle down!" Zeno ordered the adrenaline-filled dwarf. "You're making us all more nervous."

"One of those gravitron threads could wipe us out any second, and you want me to calmly stand here? I think not." Ivan started his pacing again. His forehead dripped with sweat.

Thrax ordered him off the bridge. "Go down to Engineering and double-check the Star Engines."

"I've already checked them five times!"

"Well, *settle down*, or you can go check 'em the sixth time."

Ivan must have seen the menacing look on the first officer's face, for he decided to comply. Now was not the time for a test of wills with Zeno Thrax.

Nearby, Raina and Bronwen Llewellen were manning the navigation computer console. "What do you think, Bronwen?" Raina murmured.

Bronwen was still concentrating on locating the position of the gravitron threads.

The navigator's eyes narrowed, and her voice was barely audible. "If one of those gravitron threads passes through either ship . . ." She did not finish.

Raina caught her breath. "It will blow the ships up, won't it?"

"That's right."

"I wish there were something we could *do*."

"There is. We can pray."

Pacing again, Ivan Petroski snorted. "Pray! What good will that do?"

"'More things are wrought by prayer than this world dreams of,'" Bronwen said quietly.

"That *sounds* good, anyway. Did you make it up?" Petroski asked, his eyes fixed on the monitor.

"No, it was written by an English poet named Tennyson a long time ago."

"It's a *poem?*" Petroski snorted again. "You can't run a ship on poetry!"

Bronwen smiled at him. "Man shall not live by spaceships alone."

"I like it—the poem, I mean. Do you know the rest of it?" Raina asked.

"Oh, yes. I memorized it a long time ago."

"Say it for me, will you?"

Bronwen spoke softly the ancient words.

"More things are wrought by prayer
Than this world dreams of. Wherefore, let thy voice
Rise like a fountain for me night and day.
For what are men better than sheep or goats
That nourish a blind life within the brain,
If, knowing God, they lift not hands of prayer
Both for themselves and for those who call them friend?
For so the whole round earth is every way
Bound by gold chains about the feet of God."

Petroski seemed impressed despite himself, but he had the usual male problem of wanting to appear tough. "Those are pretty words," he said. "But if the gravitron threads hit the ship, it'll go up."

"Chief," Raina said, "I don't expect you to understand, but we believe that God is greater than the threads, the black hole, the Rainbow Nebula—and the whole universe. There is nothing too hard for Him. He can do anything."

"So you're telling me that God won't let us get blown up because you've asked Him not to?"

Bronwen continued to adjust switches. "What

we're saying is, whether we live or die is totally in God's hands now. You think praying is foolishness. I think it's the smartest thing we can do."

Petroski stared at Bronwen Llewellen. He probably had great admiration for her, as did everyone else on board the *Daystar*, and secretly envied her calm faith in God. Finally he shrugged and said, "Well, you better be right. Because if God *doesn't* stop the gravitron threads, both ships are going to blow up—or be sucked into that black hole. And there's no way out of a black hole. The gravity's so strong that even light can't escape."

Raina worked steadily by Bronwen's side. Sometimes the communications equipment managed to pick up on certain frequencies that the scanners overlooked, and she was hopeful that she could do something to help the boarding party.

The array of instrument lights surrounding the navigational console was almost as dazzling as the Rainbow Nebula itself. The ship's scanners were using the console to locate any possible variant of the gravitron threads. But whenever it seemed a thread was located, it would disappear from view. The bridge crew worked feverishly trying to implement different variations of frequencies that would better locate the threads.

When Petroski went off to check the power flow registers, Bronwen suddenly said, "Raina, I've been very concerned about Jerusha—even before this rescue effort."

Raina shot a quick glance at the older woman. "I guess I haven't thought much about her. I've been more concerned about Dr. Cole. This *Wellington* mission is not going to be an easy one for her. It must be hard to face somebody who has ruined your life."

"There's not much privacy in our little world, is there?" Bronwen said. "Everyone knows the doctor's bad experience with Captain Murphy."

"He must not be much of a man to throw her to the wolves like that—just to save his own skin."

"Well, let's not be too quick to judge, Raina."

"I'm not being too quick. Everyone knows he was the one responsible for the tragedy. But instead of standing up to it like a man, he threw all the blame on Temple. You know that's not right."

"No. And yet I've done some profoundly selfish things myself."

Raina stared at her. "I don't believe it."

"Do you really think I never did anything wrong?"

As a matter of fact, Raina had almost reached the point of believing exactly that. In all the months that she had known Bronwen Llewellen, she had never seen one selfish act or heard one unkind word. Raina said with shock, "I don't think you could ever betray your friends!"

"No one knows what's in another's heart. As a matter of fact, no man knows his *own* heart—and no woman either."

"Yes, the Bible does say that."

"It also says, 'The heart is more deceitful than all else and desperately sick. Who can understand it?'"

Bronwen seemed to go back in thought. "All we can do when we commit some awful thing is to recognize what we have done and ask God's forgiveness."

"I do that, of course," Raina said. "But sometimes, Bronwen, when I'm in bed and almost asleep, a memory will come to me of some really bad thing I did. And it will be as clear as if it were yesterday—no matter if it was ten years before—and I feel the most awful guilt, even though I've confessed it and asked God's forgiveness."

106

"That's the enemy's favorite tool—to bring guilt on us. But those of us who have been saved by the blood of Jesus don't have to listen to that."

"So what do I do when those awful memories come back?"

Bronwen turned to her. "Tell Satan to take his accusation to Jesus. That He's handling your case now." She laughed aloud. "That'll cause him to go slinking off. He knows our sins were paid for on Calvary once and for all."

"What a wonderful thing. I never thought of it that way," Raina marveled. She smiled then and said, "Wait until that old Devil comes to accuse me next time!"

Suddenly she cried, "Look, Bronwen! The scanners have picked up a thick concentration of gravitron threads—and they're all headed straight for the *Wellington!*"

Bronwen struck the button on her belt. "Captain Edge, you have less than twenty minutes to get back to the *Daystar!* The rescue team must leave *Wellington*—*now!*"

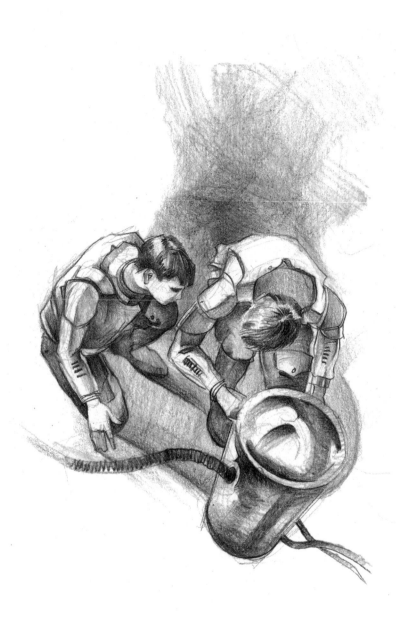

12

The Fat's in the Fire!

Ivan Petroski was in Engineering, preparing the *Daystar* for immediate Star Drive. His hands moved rapidly over the controls as if on a grand piano. In effect, the skills of Petroski were no less than those of a master musician, for to him all of the *Daystar* was an instrument and he was the artist.

Unexpectedly, the sound of low-pitched voices came to him over the hum of the engines. He cocked his head to one side. He listened carefully, and then he started stealthily down the corridor. The door to the fuel cell area was slightly ajar. When he came to the door, he saw Heck Jordan and Ringo Smith bending over something, but he could not make it out.

Ivan tiptoed into the compartment and stopped only a few feet behind the two young Rangers. And then a wave of anger rushed through him.

"What is this!" he yelled. He shoved the two aside and picked up the cable that was connected from the fuel cells to a machine that he had never seen before. His eyes blazed. "What *is* this contraption?"

Ringo looked ready to sink into the floor, and Heck was little better off. It was Heck who finally stammered a response. "Well . . . well . . . you see, Ch-Chief, it's a little something we've been working on."

"I can see that, and I can see where you've been stealing power! You've known about our power loss all the time! I'm not surprised at you, Jordan—but, Smith, I am disappointed in your joining in with this idiot!"

"Now, wait a minute, Chief. You don't know what this is!" Heck cried.

"I certainly don't. What is it?"

"It's a holographic virtual reality pod. It's going to be the greatest invention of the age." Heck seemed unable to get his words out fast enough.

But Ivan Petroski was not interested in hearing about any invention of Heck Jordan's. "I haven't got time to take care of you right now, but you'll answer for this—both of you!" He pulled the energy cable plug out of the fuel cell receptacle. The blue pod turned dark for lack of energy. "I can't begin to imagine how you two can work on this thing while the *Daystar* is in such danger. Now, come on and help me in Engineering. We've got to get ready for Star Drive capability." He gave them both a hard look, then nodded with satisfaction. "I imagine Captain Edge himself will deal with you two. This is probably your last mission on this ship."

As Petroski stalked away, Ringo gasped, "Well, the fat's in the fire now, Heck."

"Aw, we'll get out of it."

"I don't think so. We've broken about every rule in the book. And you know how Captain Edge is about breaking rules."

"Don't sweat it," Heck told him with perhaps far more confidence than he felt. "We'll get out of this somehow. See if I'm not right."

Ringo knew that Heck Jordan never worried about trouble until it closed about his head. He had seemed terrified enough when Petroski found them. But as for Captain Edge—well, Heck would figure Captain Edge was busy. In a day or two it would all be over, and he'd be rich.

Ringo Smith did not have Heck's ability to block

trouble out of his mind. A black cloud seemed to settle over him, and he thought desperately, *What will I do? They'll throw both of us off the ship for sure, and I'll have to beg for a living. I couldn't get a job anywhere! I've failed at everything I've ever tried to do.* He thought briefly of his father, Sir Richard Irons, and realized immediately that there was no help there. *Besides, I wouldn't go to him if I were dying*, he thought grimly.

After Ivan set Heck and Ringo to work in Engineering, he slipped back to secretly examine their pod. He could only guess at its purpose, but despite himself he was tremendously impressed with both boys' ability to create electronic machinery with bits and pieces of stolen equipment.

"If those two would only turn their talents to something worthwhile," he muttered, "they could do anything they wanted to." He shook his head. "They're better than they know, but I'd never tell them that."

He whirled about and stalked down the corridor until he found Studs Cagney. "Cagney, I want you to place a guard for me."

"A guard over what?"

"Something that needs to be guarded!" Petroski snapped. "Don't ask questions!" He took Cagney to the pod and said, "Don't let *anybody* get near this thing. Especially don't let anybody connect that cord to the fuel cells."

"All right, Chief." Studs was probably curious, but he shrugged.

As Petroski left, he could hear Cagney muttering, "I wonder what *this* is all about?"

"Jerusha, we have to leave! *Now!*" Captain Edge

shouted back to Jerusha as he helped Tara Jaleel with Sandoval.

The ensign was barely aware of Edge's voice. She was looking at *Wellington*'s captain, who lay slumped on the floor. His lips quivered, and his fear-filled eyes rolled from side to side. He was still clawing at the deck, trying to escape.

"Lord, please help us," Jerusha kept repeating. "Lord, Your Word says that if I humble myself before You, I can resist the Devil and he has to flee from me. Lord, I humble myself before You. Please forgive me for being mad at You. I know I was wrong. My family experience is Your responsibility, and I acknowledge that all You do is right. I don't have to understand." Jerusha felt tears rolling down her face. "Lord, we need Your help. I don't know what Satan is doing here, but I do resist him and all his wicked forces. And Your Word says that greater is He that is in me than he that is in the world—"

"Ensign, I ordered you back to the ship!" the captain yelled from the corridor. "Now *move it!*"

Jerusha *couldn't* move.

Captain Edge ran back, picked her up, and slung her over his shoulder. She glimpsed Tara Jaleel lifting Captain Murphy and placing him on *her* shoulder. Then Edge and Jaleel bolted into the corridor.

In *Daystar*'s prep room next to the air lock, Temple Cole was examining Brian Sandoval. He kept loudly praising the Lord that he had been rescued.

"Mr. Sandoval, could you *please* hold still for a few minutes? I can't get an accurate medical scan." The doctor signaled to two grunts that were standing by. "Please just hold him down so I can complete my work."

"I'm fine. In fact, I'm great! Praise the Lord." Sandoval's face gleamed with happiness.

The burly young grunts, part of the crew that did the physical labor aboard *Daystar*, had arms resembling tree trunks. When they grabbed Sandoval, he apparently knew better than to do anything but lie still. He was still laughing.

After a few minutes, Dr. Cole finished Sandoval's scan. "I can't be sure of the accuracy of this scanner right now, but it appears you are only suffering from high potency adrenaline surge. It should dissipate shortly." The doctor nodded at the grunts, who let Sandoval go and stood back, awaiting further orders.

Just then the door to the air lock burst open, and Captain Edge and Tara Jaleel staggered into the prep room, carrying Jerusha and another officer from the *Wellington*.

The captain deposited Jerusha on a bench and got on the intercom. "Edge to Thrax."

"Go ahead, Captain."

"Engage Star Drive and get us out of here."

The mighty Mark Five Star Drive engines roared to life. Normally, they were brought up to full speed slowly, but this time, despite Ivan's cautions, they were brought up to full speed at once. The *Daystar* strained under the load. These engines could easily torque the ship in half, causing an explosion that would be seen two sectors away. But, although the strain was great, the inertia stabilizers soon smoothed out *Daystar's* abrupt departure.

Temple Cole stood looking down at the *Wellington* captain. She had recognized him at once. And long-standing bitterness sent a surge of anger and resentment through her, along with a vengeful sense of satisfaction at the man's sad condition.

Captain Edge came close and whispered in her ear. "You've got to help him, Temple."

She looked back over her shoulder at him. "How can you ask me to help the man who lied to me and threw me to the dogs to save his own skin? A man who is responsible for the death of hundreds!"

"I know, Temple. But you have to help him."

"And why should I have to help him?"

"Because it's the right thing to do," he said quietly. "You have to do the right thing, or this will poison the rest of your life." Then he said, "Temple, many times I've thought of looking up this guy and stripping his skin off inch by inch because of what he did to you." He looked down at Captain Murphy. "But look at him. Whatever he's done, he doesn't deserve this."

Temple took a long, deep breath. A mighty war was raging in her heart. The memory of many dead faces flooded her mind.

She retorted hotly, "None of his victims had any chance of rescue. They died horribly of the Ebolithrax virus. Have you ever seen anyone die from Ebolithrax virus?"

"No. But does that make any difference? You told me yourself that you had no way to help them. But you *might* be able to help Murphy."

Temple Cole thought that Toland Murphy was possibly the worst human being she had ever known, but Edge was right. No one deserved this.

Looking up at the two grunts, she said, "Take him to sick bay."

Jerusha lay on a bench in the prep room. She had made no attempt to remove her enviro-suit. In fact, she'd made no movement at all except that her chest moved as she breathed.

While Edge was busy with Dr. Cole, Jerusha sensed that Tara Jaleel was trying to help her out of her suit. When Tara removed the headpiece, Jerusha weakly grabbed her wrist.

"Thank you, Tara."

Jaleel instinctively pulled back. Then, apparently, she decided that she was in no danger.

Jerusha looked up into Jaleel's eyes. The darkness she saw in them was almost as black as the black hole of the Rainbow Nebula.

Tara finished unfastening all the enviro-suit fittings. "There, *child*. You can undo the rest yourself."

Jaleel walked out of the prep room, throwing her own enviro-suit at one of the grunts.

Jerusha thought for a moment and decided to pray. "Lord, somehow, some way, please help Tara Jaleel."

13

Daystar in Danger

"Turn the recorders on—I have no doubt that Commandant Lee will want to see this," Captain Edge instructed Raina St. Clair. "Mr. Thrax," he continued. "Turn up magnification sixty percent. *Wellington* is getting hard to see at normal levels."

Zeno adjusted the controls so that the main viewer enlarged the Magnum Deep Space Cruiser. The albino looked up at Captain Edge, and a small tear came to his eye.

Captain Edge put a hand on his first officer's shoulder. "It should be any time now."

The bridge crew watched the viewer in amazement and dismay as a cluster of gravitron threads sliced through *Wellington* like a hot knife through butter. The great ship was literally carved into pieces, each of which started its journey toward the black hole of the Rainbow Nebula. They had witnessed the death of one of Intergalactic Command's mighty starships.

Captain Edge's forehead creased as he thought of the lost crew. And then the captain surprised himself by wanting to tell a story.

"One of my earliest memories," he said, "is the time my family went white-water canoeing. I was ten, and my brother John was six."

Edge walked to his chair without taking his eyes off the disintegrating Magnum Deep Space Cruiser. Then he looked down at the crew. All eyes were still watching the *Wellington* on the viewer, but he knew that they were listening to his every word. Mark Edge rarely shared his past with them. And certainly not at a time like this.

Remembering the event as though it had just happened, he went on. "The first day was so enjoyable. Clear water, blue sky with small puffs of white clouds. Warm and nice. Flowering trees blanketing the valley with white and pink. Every once in a while we'd pass bushes that were a beautiful dark yellow. John and I played at trying to drench each other. My brother knew just how to hit the water with his paddle to get me sopping wet. Then we came to some rapids. Mostly they were pretty slow and tame."

Edge sat in his command chair and gazed up at the ceiling, recalling the day. "We shot through several small rapids. My dad praised me for my boatmanship. I was getting pretty cocky. In fact, I felt *invincible!*

"The next morning, Dad went fishing—he caught three rainbow trout. We had them for breakfast. Over the years, I've decided that was the best breakfast I ever had."

Edge became silent for a few moments, and a cloud came over his face. "Dad started helping Mom pack up the camping gear so we could start on the next leg of the trip. My brother and I were messing around with one of the canoes." He stopped to clear his throat. "I never realized how powerful the current could be. I pushed the canoe out into the water only a little bit—I was just trying to scare him. The canoe left my hand for only a second. But that second was enough for the current to whisk the canoe—and my brother—right out into the middle of the river. It happened so fast. One second, he's right there with me; the next second, he's fifty feet downstream. I yelled at my dad for help."

Edge got up and walked to the forward part of the

bridge. He fell silent again as he stared at the gravitron threads.

"And then what happened?" It was Raina who asked.

"He was standing up in the canoe, waving his arms at us. My dad dove into the stream and swam toward him as fast as he could. My mother was screaming for my little brother to sit down. He didn't. Maybe he didn't hear her. And then the canoe hit a rock. It threw him out of the canoe into the rapids."

Edge rubbed his forehead. "That was the last time I saw my dad and my brother alive. The park rangers found them later—about two miles downstream."

The bridge crew was silent. The only noise to be heard was the droning of the computers and the Star Drive engines.

Captain Edge looked around at his crew. He felt a closeness to all of them. "I didn't wake up that day with the thought that Dad and John would die—and that I would be responsible! I was cocky. I had just *whipped* the river the day before. What could go wrong?"

Edge walked back to his command chair, patting Zeno on the shoulder as he passed.

"But, Captain"—Raina spoke up again—"none of you could have known that was going to happen."

"My mom and I understood that. But understanding didn't make it any easier for us. Each of us blamed ourselves. My family life was never the same after that day."

He nodded toward the dismembered *Wellington* on the viewer. "One morning a few days ago, none of the seven hundred persons aboard the *Wellington* woke up and said to themselves that this was the day they were going to die. But they did die. This black hole, this beautiful Rainbow Nebula, and even the gravitron threads are part of nature. I learned that you *never* whip nature—you respect it. Most of the time, it will let you journey through life with no problems. But watch out—nature's rapids could be around the next bend, and you'd better be prepared for them.

"I don't have any idea why the *Wellington* was ordered into this part of space, but I hope no one is ever sent here again. This is definitely a part of nature that is best left alone!"

"Captain, what else?" Jerusha asked then. "I sense you're not telling us everything you meant to say."

Edge's eyes suddenly were teary. "What I'm trying to say is—look around you! I lost my real family years ago, and I've never had another until now—all of you. We're out here in the heart of deep space, and we're all we've got. We've got to hold onto each other the best that we can and never let go. We came very close to winding up just like the *Wellington*. We almost lost each other for good. I just want you to think about that."

He looked around at each person and then started for the corridor. "First, you have the bridge," he said as he went out.

"Aye, Captain."

As a result of *Daystar*'s entering the Rainbow Nebula, Dr. Temple Cole had her sick bay crowded to capacity. An epidemic of terrible headaches had struck many of the crew. Jerusha, Heck, Ringo, Raina, three of the grunts, and Ivan Petroski had all staggered in, complaining of blinding headaches.

"I've heard of migraines," Jerusha gasped. "If they're worse than this, I don't see how people live through them."

"You're going to be all right, Jerusha." Dr. Cole was

standing beside the cot where the girl lay absolutely still. "Try not to move. It'll soon pass away."

Temple moved along to where Heck Jordan lay flat on his back, his eyes closed, and his face as pale as she had ever seen it. "Are you doing all right, Heck?"

"Am I going to die?"

"No, of course not."

"Oh! That's a disappointment."

Temple could not help grinning. The boy, for all his faults, was able at times to laugh at himself. She brushed back his hair. "I know it hurts, but the medication will kick in soon."

Heck held up his hand and opened his eyes a slit. "Will I be able to play the piano?"

"Of course you will."

Heck managed a grin. "That's funny. I never could play before."

Dr. Cole could not hold back a burst of laughter. "You're not as sick as you might be. You lie still."

When she got to Ivan, she reassured him that the headaches were only a side effect and that he would soon feel better.

The diminutive chief moaned. "My head hurts so bad I can't even think straight. It's like someone's driving a spike from temple to temple."

"You'll be all right, Ivan. Just lie still."

"What's the story on this Captain Murphy, Doc?"

Temple Cole bit her lip. She hated medical problems that she could not solve, and, of course, there were many of them. "I'm not sure," she said slowly. "Somehow he's locked inside his mind and can't find his way out. He seems to be groping around in his subconscious . . ."

Ivan grunted. "Sounds terrible. I'd rather get a

physical wound. Isn't there any way you could look inside his head and help him?"

"Medicine hasn't gone quite that far yet, Chief."

Then Heck Jordan called out faintly, "Hey, Doc, come here."

Temple moved back to Heck. "What is it? Is the pain worse?"

"No, but I just thought of something. I've been working on a new invention that's going to make me rich and famous."

"Again?" She smiled. "Is this the fiftieth or the six-tieth?"

"You go ahead and laugh, but one of these days, Doc, you'll be saying, 'Well, I knew Mr. Jordan before he was the greatest man in the galaxy.' But let me tell you about what I've done. I've made a holographic vir-tual reality pod." He went on to explain how his inven-tion worked.

Temple thought, *This is the most absurd thing I've ever heard of—even from Heck. And why is he telling me all this?*

But Heck was still talking. "I meant the pod for playing out fantasies. You know—like the old movies except that you're really in them."

"What does this have to do with Captain Murphy, Heck?"

"Well, I thought somehow you could use it to get into his mind."

"How would I do that?"

"I don't know. But I'm telling you, it's a powerful thing."

"I think he may be right, Dr. Cole."

Temple turned. On the cot behind her, Ringo had raised himself on one elbow. Perspiration burst out on his forehead, and she could tell that he was hurting badly.

"Lie down again, Ringo." She forced him back down and then held her hand to his forehead. "What do you know about all this?"

"Well, I did some of the work," Ringo admitted. "In fact, Captain Edge is probably going to throw us both off the ship for breaking the rules."

"He'd never do that."

"You don't think so?"

"Of course not."

"Well, I don't know much about medicine, but I know Heck's principles are sound. And I think it's possible that the same principle that would allow a mind to enter a dream . . . well, you might get inside the captain's mind and find out what's going on in there."

"Do you really think it would work?"

"The tridium crystals are absolutely unique, Dr. Cole. Who knows what all can be done with them? But it sounds like Captain Murphy is going to die if something isn't done, and quick!"

Slowly Temple Cole nodded. "I'm afraid you're right. Well, you lie still now. You'll be feeling better soon."

Dr. Cole moved away, but her mind was busily at work with the problem. She turned it one way and another. For some time she scoffed at herself for even considering using an invention of Heck Jordan's. *He's about the most selfish person on this ship—or anywhere else that I know of*, she thought. *What does he have to contribute?*

But as she struggled with the problem of how to help the dying captain, one thought came to her clearly: *If there were any other way, I wouldn't even think of it. But as far as I can see, Heck Jordan's virtual reality pod is the only chance that Captain Murphy has. I'll have to talk to Mark about this.*

Filling her hypos with the headache cure, Dr. Cole treated everyone in sick bay. Before the end of the day, all the headaches were gone, and the crew members were back at their workstations.

14

Someone Always Has It Worse

Ivan Petroski picked up the power coupling that connected the fuel cells directly to Heck's holographic virtual reality machine.

Like all his people, when Ivan was nervous, he was completely honest about how he felt. "Captain, being this close to the fuel cells is dangerous," he complained. "We don't really know what this thing does."

"Ivan, go ahead and hook it up. We have to take the chance. Dr. Cole told me that if we don't get Captain Murphy's adrenaline levels back down to normal, he will die. This contraption is the only hope we have." Captain Edge's forehead creased with worry lines. He didn't want his ship to blow up, but try as he might, he could think of no other plan to help Murphy.

He walked around to the doorway that led into the blue pod. Inside, Heck Jordan was working away, and Dr. Cole was busy strapping Captain Murphy to the holograph's body frame. Any movement by Captain Murphy would register on the supercomputer, and Murphy would see himself moving around on the screen just as if the whole fantasy were real. The brain sensors were the most critical part of the machine. If they weren't tuned just right, the whole thing could permanently damage Murphy's already deteriorating mental condition.

"Mark," the doctor said, "I have him strapped into this thing, but I'm certainly not sure any of this is going to work. I've no reason to think it *will* work!"

"Don't feel bad, Temple. This whole thing is a bizarre experiment. My only concerns are that we can help Murphy and not blow up the *Daystar* in the process. I just wish we had a little more time."

Edge walked on into the pod. Holographic emitters were embedded in the ceiling, floor, and all the walls. He examined the sensors that Temple was about to place at the base of Murphy's neck. "Tridium! Heck, you stole some of my tridium!"

Heck kept adjusting the emitters. "Naw, I only borrowed it. This mineral is the future. You have no idea how powerful it is, Captain Edge. Tridium will revolutionize science as we know it."

Edge responded angrily, "I'll revolutionize *you!* Ensign Jordan, when this is over, I want you to return every gram of tridium back to me."

Heck smiled a big smile. "Captain, when I explain a few things to you, you'll thank me for using it."

Cole came up to Edge, wrapped her arm in his, and pulled him away from the Ranger. She placed her lips very close to the captain's ear. "Mark, cut Heck a little slack. If it weren't for his 'experimenting,' Murphy would have no chance at all."

Edge glared back at Heck, but he tried to hide his anger. In spite of the serious nature of what Heck had done, when Temple Cole made a request, Mark Edge would have done anything she asked.

"Heck, we'll talk about this later. For right now, you have free rein to use whatever materials you need. Just make this thing work!"

Dr. Cole did a further medical scan on Murphy. While she was passing the scanner across his face, she found herself thinking, *This is not the face of the arrogant, self-centered Toland Murphy that I knew. This face is the real face of Captain Murphy—alone and fearful.*

Bronwen Llewellen came into the pod just then. "He doesn't look like the Devil anymore, does he?" she said quietly.

"No, he doesn't. Not at all."

Murphy's body was limp, and his eyes darted in all directions. Sometimes his head would jerk, causing his long silver hair to fly in disarray.

"I imagine Captain Murphy has always been a lonely man," Bronwen said. "He may never have known real love—either for himself, for other people, or especially for God. He's achieved a lot in his life, but at the expense of others. You weren't the first person he betrayed, Temple. He didn't love you—he used you. He would sacrifice anyone to benefit himself."

"Bronwen, how can you know all this?"

"Two ways. First, I've been around the galaxy a few times, and you learn certain things during the trip. Second, the Lord has been speaking to my heart about him. The Lord loves him and has compassion on him. We can do no less."

"I don't have the strength of your convictions about God yet, but I do know that's the right thing to do. Jerusha told me that we can't return evil for evil. The Murphy I knew was the king of his domain, the mighty captain of a mighty ship. The Murphy in front of me now . . ." Tears started streaming down Temple's cheeks. Her moments of closeness with Toland Murphy were replaying themselves in her mind.

Perhaps Bronwen sensed Temple's feelings for the *Wellington* captain. "Temple . . . it's OK to feel love for this man, selfish as he was."

Temple looked at Bronwen. "I do love him, but not in the same way I did before."

127

Bronwen stroked back Murphy's hair from his face. "I'm not saying that I've mastered this. But Jesus tells us that we should love our enemies and do good to those who would hurt us. In our universe, people are centered on themselves. Instead of helping each other, they crush others—people who have the same faults they do."

Temple reflected. "And I'm not any different, either. That's terrible, isn't it?"

Bronwen took her hand. "None of us is different, none of us is noble, none of us is pure and good." She took a kerchief from her pocket and handed it to Temple. "What *is* different about Christians is that Jesus Himself lives in them. And He is the One who makes Christians a different sort of people."

Temple wiped the tears from her eyes. "Ever since I've been on this ship, things have happened—people have said things that affected me and, deep down inside of me, things have been going on . . ."

Bronwen took Murphy's hand in her own. Now she was holding Temple's hand in her left hand and Captain Murphy's in her right. "The captain has the same need that you do. He needs to acknowledge that Jesus Christ is his Lord and Savior—and so do you, Temple."

In a way that had never happened to her before, a light seemed to turn on in her head. She suddenly understood her condition—she was lost! She realized now that her life had seemed so empty because Jesus was not in it. She had tried to fill the void with other things, but couldn't do it. Only Jesus could.

"Bronwen, could you help me?"

And then Bronwen helped Temple Cole pray the sinner's prayer. She confessed that she had indeed sinned against God, and then she told Jesus Christ that she accepted Him as her Lord and her Savior.

As Temple looked up and smiled at Bronwen Llewellen, she knew in the deep part of her heart that she had been changed forever.

Ivan came into the pod then. "Everybody out. I'm firing up the supercomputer."

"I'll be finished in a second," Heck barked at him.

Petroski turned and left, mumbling things under his breath.

Captain Edge was still standing outside the pod when Ivan and then Bronwen came out. "Captain, I know this is not what we agreed upon," she said. "But instead of Zeno or Jerusha hooking into the hologram with Captain Murphy, I think it should be Dr. Cole."

"But either Zeno and Jerusha is better able to . . . to *sense* things in people. Just getting that albino friend of mine to agree to do this was a major effort. I had to call in every personal favor I've ever done for him."

"Then he should have no problem being relieved of this responsibility."

"But why?"

"Because Temple is in a unique position to help Captain Murphy now. Murphy won't know Jerusha. And the sight of Zeno may scare the daylights out of him."

Edge glanced over at Zeno Thrax, who really did look quite scary to those who didn't know him. "I see what you mean, but why *Temple?* This thing might fry her brains, and I don't want that to happen. To her or to anybody!"

"None of us do." But Bronwen's face took on a look of determination. "In my opinion, Captain, Temple was a way out of a tough situation for Murphy once. When he sees her in the hologram, he will probably want to use her that way again. You must let Temple be the one who contacts him."

When Dr. Cole exited the pod, Edge went to her. "Bronwen says you should be the one to interact with Murphy in the hologram."

"I'm scared of what may happen, Mark, but I too think that I'm the right choice. It's important for *me* to do it."

Edge nodded slowly in agreement, then reluctantly walked over to the pod door and shouted to Heck. "Heck, reconfigure the computer for Dr. Cole. She's the one going in."

"Aye, sir."

At the faked tone of respect, Captain Edge determined that he was going to do everything he could to get Heck's attention after this was over. *If Heck thinks he's had it bad with Tara Jaleel,* he thought, *just wait till I get through with him.*

The moment they had all prepared for had arrived. Heck, Ringo, and Ivan had adjusted the supercomputer so that it would display on the viewer outside the pod everything that was happening inside.

Heck helped Dr. Cole hook herself up to the second electro-skeletal sensor array. "The neck sensors are the most important," she said. "Are you sure they're right?"

"You checked them yourself, Doctor. We've adjusted them the best we can. This is new technology, and it hasn't been tested yet. What do you want me to say?"

Temple walked over to stand beside Captain Murphy, who was still in a seated position. As Heck went out, closing the pod door, she waved at Ivan to start the hologram. She looked down at the sensors connected to her fingers and arms. The room turned dark.

"Go away, whoever you are! There's no room in

here for anyone but me!" The strained voice of Captain Murphy spoke suddenly and fiercely from out of the dimness.

"Toland, where are you?" Temple inquired gently. She was very aware of how fragile his mind was.

"Who is it?" he asked in a milder tone.

"It's me . . . Temple Cole."

"Temple? I don't believe you. This is just another ruse by those infernal . . . creatures!" His voice turned harsh again.

As Temple's eyes slowly became accustomed to the gloom, she could make out his figure sitting in the far corner of the pod.

"Don't come any closer," Murphy said threateningly.

"Toland, it's really me. There's no one here but us. I don't see any creatures."

Slowly, the captain's dark shape began to brighten, and then muted colors started to become visible. Finally, Toland Murphy's seated form came into full view.

"What are you doing here? Come back for a little revenge?" he asked tersely.

There was no hint of love in his voice. She heard only the tone of hatred.

"I'm here to help you, Toland. But you've got to help me help you."

The *Wellington* captain laughed. "You couldn't even help yourself. How are you going to help me? Besides, you're one of *them* anyway, and I know what you really want."

"Listen, listen to me. I really am Temple." The doctor had to use all her experience to remain patient and encouraging. "Toland," she went on, "I think you've hidden yourself in a special place inside your heart.

Somewhere that you feel safe." She took a step toward him.

"Stop! I'm warning you!" Murphy screamed at her.

"Toland, you must let me help you. Tell me—what is the last thing you remember?"

"I was on the bridge of the *Wellington,* that's what! You should know. You guys were all around me."

In response to Murphy's remembering, abruptly the holograph pod was transformed in appearance to the *Wellington*'s bridge. Brian Sandoval stood in the background, working feverishly on several control consoles. A screaming Murphy was trying to claw through the bridge bulkhead. The bridge itself was crawling with the ugliest creatures that Temple had ever seen. They looked as though a vampire bat, a lizard, and a monkey had had their DNA codes scrambled, and the resulting combination had produced these hideous beasts.

Then, suddenly, a portal of fire opened on the holographic bridge. The beasts seized the captain and began dragging him toward the fiery door.

"Get away! Get away!" Murphy yelled. If they pulled him through, there was no way out.

"Help me, Temple!"

On the outside viewer, Captain Edge and the bridge crew stood watching in fascination. Suddenly the holographic bridge turned back into its original dimness. The creatures were gone. The fiery door was gone. All they could see on the viewer was Temple Cole. Then Murphy reappeared faintly, hiding in a corner.

Jerusha whispered to Bronwen, "I understand exactly what Murphy is doing. I have one of those rooms in my heart, too."

Bronwen responded quietly, "We all do." She took

Jerusha's hand in her own and squeezed it as they followed the action on the viewer.

Despite his warnings, Temple walked to where Murphy was sitting.

His eyes, fearful, were still darting back and forth, up and down.

Gently, Temple took him by the shoulders.

Murphy offered no resistance. "What are you looking for?" he asked anxiously. "*I'm* looking for the way out. I've always been able to find a way out when I come in here, but now I can't find it."

The surroundings shifted in the holographic pod, and Murphy's form took on more shape and color again. His memory was activating a change of scene.

Temple and Murphy were traveling in an air car out in the country. She remembered the day. It was early summer. The air was pleasant and warm. Murphy had just lowered the top of the vehicle, and the wind was blowing her curly hair.

"Toland, I don't know how you talked me into spending a weekend out in the country with you." She wore a big smile as she tried to hold her hair down.

Murphy turned and smiled back at her.

The scene on the viewer looked the same to Temple as it had that day five years ago when she had let herself fall in love with him. But this time she was able to understand the captain's true intentions.

This time she saw that Murphy knew she was infatuated with him. She was the next girl out of many, another notch on his gun. As captain of a starship, women pursued him. Temple had been his hardest target in a long time. But at last she had confirmed to him that women eventually were suckers for a handsome face, money, and power.

That was enough for Temple. She decided to put a stop to this holographic scene. Concentrating very hard, she changed the scene back to the dim pod.

"Toland, this won't help you. We are not in the air car. That was five years ago. Today we are in your dark room. You are looking for a way out. Remember?"

Murphy shook his head slightly and looked up. "Temple, this is really you, isn't it?"

"Yes, it's really me. I've brought you a gift. Something that you need to get out of here."

His eyes darted back and forth. "Brought me what? I don't see anything."

Temple concentrated again, taking control of the virtual reality program herself. A door appeared in the center of the pod. The door was ajar.

"Toland, this is your escape door. Take my hand. I can't carry you through the escape door. You have to walk through it yourself."

"No!" he screamed. "It's a trap!"

Very calmly Temple assured him, "Toland, the door you see is your way of escape. You *have* to walk through it."

"I can stay right here. I don't have to go anywhere."

"Listen to me. If you don't come out right now, through that door, you will die. Do you want to die in here?"

He looked in all directions. He replied, "No, I don't."

Temple took his hand and helped him stand. Then, step by step, Murphy made his way to the holographic door. Slowly it opened of its own accord. On the other side of the door a light shone, a beautiful light that was warm and nourishing to the heart.

"What *is* this, Temple?" he asked cautiously.

"All I can tell you is that this same light is in my heart—where my dark room used to be. God put His light there, and He wants to place His light in your heart, too. His door is the only door for you. There are no others."

At first Captain Murphy said he was afraid of the light. He wanted the safety of the dark. But soon the light reached out to him. Gentle arms of light embraced him.

"I've never felt anything like this," Murphy said. "This light feels so warm, so good . . ."

Temple smiled at him. "Don't be afraid," she reassured him.

Murphy seemed to know exactly what to say next. Looking through the door, he said, "God, if that's You, I'm sorry for messing up everything all these years. I've hurt so many people. Please forgive me! I don't know if You're willing, but for Jesus' sake . . ."

Murphy stretched out both arms and walked through the door.

In a flash of blinding light, the images were gone. The holographic pod shut down. Captain Murphy and Temple Cole were once again surrounded by the sky blue walls of Heck Jordan's virtual reality machine.

Captain Edge and his staff sat spellbound. None of them seemed able to utter a word for a few minutes. What they had just experienced was far beyond anything that any of them had expected.

And then Bronwen, Dai, and Raina all shouted, "Praise the Lord!" at the same time.

Jerusha's voice followed with, "Amen."

As Jerusha and Bronwen walked away from the holographic pod area, Jerusha moved closer to the navigator. "You know, Bronwen, this experience has made a big difference in my thinking."

"How is that, Jerusha?"

"I mean all of my hard feelings about not having had a family when I was growing up. Sure, my life was pretty bad, but Captain Murphy's life was worse. Well . . . his makes me appreciate my own a lot more."

"I'm glad you can feel like that, Jerusha," Bronwen said quietly. "The Lord knows what is best for each of us. He builds some things into each life that are different from anyone else's. And He uses all things for our good! The Space Rangers are your family now, and I predict that you're going to enjoy this family more now that you've got this other thing out of your mind."

"Even Heck?" Jerusha grinned.

"Especially Heck. He's got some unsettled issues in his heart, too, but God's going to deal with that."

"I suppose we all have unsettled issues," Jerusha murmured. "This has been a hard thing for me. I didn't even know it was *in* me."

"Well, you've learned to know yourself a little bit. For one thing, you've learned that self-pity makes us lose sight of the fact that there's always someone who has it a lot worse than we do."

"I know that now. I'm just sorry for the crew of the *Wellington*. I wish they could have been saved."

"We all grieve over them, though we didn't know them personally. It was a terrible thing."

Captain Edge, with Dr. Cole by his side, confronted Heck just outside the holographic pod. Edge's eyes bored into the ensign. "I had a good mind to throw you into deep space, Jordan. But I have to admit that your invention came in pretty handy after all. Especially to Captain Murphy."

"You don't know half of it, Captain," Heck boasted.

"Why, this pod can do things nobody ever thought of." He laid a hand on it.

Without warning, the virtual reality machine erupted. It spewed forth a volcano of sparkling lights. The acrid smell of burning circuitry filled the air. Edge dragged Temple back, shielding her with his body. Heck lunged away, then hit the deck, curling up into a big ball. The *Daystar*'s fire alarm sounded. The smoke evacuation unit started sucking out the smoke-filled air.

Captain Edge ran to the smoldering pod, took one look inside, then let out a yell. He grabbed his Neuromag and fired through the door.

"What was it, Mark?" Temple cried.

"It was this!" Edge exclaimed. "I never saw anything like it." Heck and Temple joined him at the pod doorway and looked down at a little white-and-beige animal.

"Why, the critter's destroyed my pod's main supercomputer. He bit through its power supply!" Heck exclaimed. His face turned pale. "Every circuit's burned to a crisp," he gasped, "and it all happened in less than a second. It'll take me months, even years, to get enough stuff to rebuild it!"

Captain Edge glared at the boy. "I'm giving you an order, Jordan. Don't you dare take any more tridium. Don't even think about it. Or I'll hand you over to Tara Jaleel!"

Heck swallowed hard and dropped his head. For once he had nothing to say.

Suddenly Edge put an arm around the chubby ensign and hugged him hard. Giving Temple a wink, he said, "You're more trouble than the rest of the crew put together, Jordan, but somewhere down deep inside of you there's a fine soldier. I just hope I'm around long enough to see it come out."

Temple leaned forward and kissed Heck on the cheek, which caused his face to turn red. "You saved Captain Murphy's life, Heck. You can always be proud of that."

Heck appeared to struggle for a moment, perhaps trying to think of some boastful remark to make. Then he looked up at the captain and said, "Aw, Captain, it wasn't all that much."

Mark and Temple looked at each other with astonishment. "I can't believe it!" Edge gasped. "Modesty!"

"Maybe," Temple said, "this is the new Heck Jordan."

"What's wrong with the old Heck Jordan?" Heck obviously had had as much modesty as he could stand. Reaching into his pocket, he pulled out three candy bars and said, "Here, you both need to put some meat on your bones."

15

Homeward Bound

The *Daystar* hurtled effortlessly through the glittering star systems. All around were diamond pinpoints of stars, stretching as far as a telescope could see.

From the bridge, Mark Edge and Temple Cole watched the Rainbow Nebula fade into the distance.

The captain looked solemnly at the disappearing nebula's black hole with its surrounding rainbow colors. "I'm glad to be leaving *that*."

"However, I'd have to say that—from a distance—that black hole has about the prettiest packaging I've ever seen," Temple commented.

"Which just proves you can't judge a book by its cover." He winked at her.

"Excuse me, but are you talking about the nebula or about something else?"

Captain Edge grinned broadly as now he looked into the doctor's eyes. "The colors of the Rainbow Nebula are beyond compare—except, of course, they don't surpass the deep violet beauty of your eyes."

Temple glanced around. The crew wisely acted as if Edge and Cole weren't even on the bridge.

Mei-Lani and Raina were off duty, and they sat in Mei-Lani's quarters. The younger girl was laughing. "It's really ridiculous the way both Heck and Ringo try to get your attention, Raina."

"I think it's ridiculous, too, and I wish they would

stop. I don't know why boys have to be such show-offs. They don't need to show off to me. It'd be better if they would just be themselves."

Mei-Lani considered that. "I don't think they will ever quit that sort of thing. It's just the way boys are."

"I suppose so, but they certainly act silly at times."

For a while they quietly sipped their melon nectar drinks, and then Mei-Lani giggled again. "Heck is telling everybody that he's going to slim down and take lessons from Dai so that he'll be physically fit."

"He needs to. Not that he'd ever be Dai's equal."

"Nobody could be that, but at least he'd be healthier. Did you see him try to turn a back flip to catch your attention this morning?"

It was Raina St. Clair's turn to giggle. "Yes, and it's a wonder he didn't break his neck."

"He was out cold as a wedge. And then Ringo tried the same thing, and he landed right on top of his head."

"They looked so funny," Mei-Lani said, "lying stretched out like that!"

"Serves them right for showing off. Girls never do things like that."

"Oh, I think girls show off, too. Just in different ways."

"What do you mean?"

"I mean when girls get to a certain age they start putting on makeup and worrying about their hair and their clothes. They're not doing it for *themselves.*"

Raina stared at her friend and finally gave a reluctant grin. "Well, that's still not as bad as turning back flips and knocking yourself out," she said.

Tara Jaleel appeared to be examining the workout room when Jerusha stepped inside.

"I'd like to hang something on the wall, Lieutenant." Jerusha's tone made her announcement sound more like a demand than a request.

Tara Jaleel nodded her head. She seemed not particularly interested.

On the bulkhead Jerusha fastened a picture of Jesus on the cross. She had painted it herself.

As the ensign stepped back and turned around, her eyes met the eyes of Tara Jaleel. Tara's were flaming. Jerusha started to say something, but she had tried her best to witness to this woman without any success whatsoever. Turning away, she left the exercise area, uttering aloud a prayer for the lieutenant. "Dear Lord, help Tara."

Tara Jaleel angrily stalked around the training room. Then she stopped, her eyes resting on the statue of Shiva she had placed in the room's most prominent position. Suddenly, in the silence, it seemed Tara could hear a *trumpet* sounding.

She knew somehow that the trumpet blast would not have been heard by anyone else on the ship. The sound was inside her own head. She began to tremble all over—an experience she had never known before.

Then, even as Jaleel watched, without warning the statue of Shiva collapsed. It was as if someone had struck the idol with a sledgehammer. It fell into a thousand pieces, and dust particles sifted like flakes of gray ash to the floor.

Tara's throat was dry, and she could not move. She could not tell if this was real or was just a vision. But for once in her life, she felt broken. Tremors swept over her body. And for the first time, Tara Jaleel began to question the power of Shiva, to whom she had entrusted her soul.

On the bridge, Raina St. Clair called for Captain Edge. "Incoming message from the *Cromwell*."

"Put it on-screen."

The face of *Cromwell*'s captain, Sam Cook, appeared on the forward viewer. This "Sam" was a woman. At five eleven, she was all business. She wore her blonde hair in braids down to the small of her back. Her eyes were steel gray, and her lips were like two thin lines drawn from cheek to cheek. Edge's boyish charms had never worked on her. He had gotten on her bad side more than once.

With a very cordial look on her face today, Captain Cook said, "Greetings, Captain. We received your message about *Wellington*. Terrible loss." She shook her head sadly. "We've been ordered to rendezvous with you and pick up Captain Murphy and Chief Engineer Sandoval. It seems that the people at Command Base Three want to debrief them on their mission."

Before Edge could speak to Bronwen, the navigator responded. "Already received and plotted, sir."

"Well, I guess we'll be seeing you in about an hour, Captain Cook," Edge said. "Could you join us for dinner?"

All business as usual, Cook replied, "Sorry, Edge. We don't have time. Command Base Three wants those two yesterday."

Turning on his boyish grin, Captain Edge asked, "What's this all about, Sam?"

But nothing about Edge could charm Cook today. "This information is classified 'need to know,'" she advised. "And you, Captain, *don't* need to know." Sam Cook glanced around her bridge, then stepped closer to her viewer. With apparently as much sincerity as she could muster, she said, "My earnest hope, Captain

Edge, is that you *never* know. Trust me on this. Cook out." The viewer went blank.

In the recreation area, Dai Bando stood beside Jerusha at the space port. Contessa sat on the floor between them. The *Cromwell* had just picked up Murphy and Sandoval. The two Space Rangers were watching one of the mightiest ships in Intergalactic Command turn into a stream of light and race into infinite blackness, headed toward Command Base Three.

Dai turned away from the window to Jerusha. "Well, another mission accomplished. And we all made it through."

"We did, and I'm grateful to the Lord for keeping us."

"You're feeling better yourself, aren't you, Jerusha?"

Jerusha stared up at him. "How did you know I was having trouble?"

"You didn't seem to be yourself. But you *are* much better now, aren't you?"

"Yes, I am. Dai, I wish I were like you. You never seem to have any trouble."

Dai shook his head. "We all have our problems."

As the two again looked out into space, Jerusha Ericson thought about what the boy had just said. Wallowing in self-pity had been her problem, and it had nearly destroyed her. Then she smiled up at him, saying, "Well, the Lord brought me through my problem. He always does."

Contessa stood up on her hind legs so that she could see out the port, too. Her tongue hanging out, she looked at the unblinking stars. "Wuff! Wuff!" she barked.

Far ahead lay the quadrant where Earth was located. There the lights of home gleamed faintly. Jerusha and Dai watched as they grew brighter and brighter.